# ENDORSEMENTS

With the control of most media, Hollywood, government, and education in the hands of the devil, few understand just how diabolical socialism is to a nation until it's too late! There has NEVER been a more important time than NOW to read this book.

Sid Roth
Host, *It's Supernatural!*

*Satan Is a Socialist* is packed full of thought-provoking information that will ROCK your political thinking! Read it before you vote again!

- Where did socialism come from?
- Who invented free enterprise?
- What is the history?
- And what is the fruit produced?

While Dr. Clark shares thought-provoking information that will rock political thinking, her down-to-earth explanations and examples...make logical sense. [Dr. Clark's] in-depth research provides fresh insight into the politic̲ ̲ ̲ ̲ ̲ ̲ ̲ ̲ ̲ ̲ ̲ ̲ ̲ ̲ ̲ ̲ortant read!

̲ ̲ ̲ ̲eview, Xulon Press

D1293318

*Satan Is a Socialist* is a powerful, myth-busting book that confronts one of the central spiritual and political issues of our time. Dr. Jennifer Clark masterfully examines Biblical and historical evidence on the kind of economic system that fosters liberty and shatters bondage and dependence.

You need this book.

Your friends need this book.

Your country needs this book.

The time has come for a new birth of freedom!

JIM BUCHAN, Crosslink Ministries
Jim Buchan has served as a pastor, an attorney, and the editor of *Ministries Today Magazine* and *The MorningStar Journal*. His articles have appeared in more than 40 publications worldwide. Jim is the author of several books, including *Apostolic Evangelism* and *Walking the Leadership Highway—Without Becoming Road Kill!*

# SATAN
## IS A
# SOCIALIST

# SATAN
## —— IS A ——
# SOCIALIST

### FREE
### ENTERPRISE
### VS. SOCIALISM

**DR. JENNIFER B. CLARK WITH
DR. DENNIS L. CLARK**

It's Supernatural! Press and Messianic Vision Inc.

Cover design by Eileen Rockwell

ISBN TP: 978-0-7684-5974-6
ISBN eBook: 978-0-7684-5853-4
ISBN PoD LP: 978-0-7684-5975-3
ISBN PoD HC: 978-0-7684-5976-0

For Worldwide Distribution, Printed in the U.S.A.
1 2 3 4 5 6 7 8 / 25 24 23 22 21

# DEDICATION

This book is dedicated to Americans and freedom lovers everywhere, young and old. May you grasp the torch of liberty and guard it as though your life depends on it—for indeed it does.

> A primary object...should be the education of our youth in the science of government. In a republic, what species of knowledge can be equally important? And what duty more pressing...than...communicating it to those who are to be the future guardians of the liberties of the country?
>
> —PRESIDENT GEORGE WASHINGTON,
> Eighth Annual Message to the Senate and
> House of Representatives, December 7, 1796

# CONTENTS

# PREFACE

Look around! It's clear that things are in a mess. Conflict, rage, destruction, riots, storms, fires, catastrophes, and confusion. It almost seems as though we are in a war between good and evil.

Wait! I believe we are!

To go back to the beginning, the origin of things in the world today, we have to go to Genesis, the book of beginnings. The trouble we're in started way back at the beginning of this world we live in. At first, in the Garden of Eden all was harmonious. People, animals, and even nature all lived without strife in a mystical perfection. The reason for all this harmony was the alignment of all things with a good God. Do not be deceived by false promises of a godless utopia without the true God.

The trouble started in Genesis 3:1-6, from the Easy-to-Read (ERV) translation of the Bible:

> *The snake was the most clever of all the wild animals that the Lord God had made. The snake spoke to the woman and said, "Woman, did God really tell you that you must not eat from any tree in the garden?" The woman answered the snake, "No, we can eat fruit from the trees in the garden. But there is one tree we must not eat from. God told us, 'You must not eat fruit from the tree that is in the middle of the garden. You must not even touch that tree, or you will die.'" But the snake said to the woman, "You will not die. God knows that if you eat the fruit from that tree you will learn about good and evil, and then you will be like God!" The woman could see that the tree was beautiful and the fruit looked so good to eat. She also liked the idea that it would make her wise. So she took some of the fruit from the tree and ate it. Her husband was there with her, so she gave him some of the fruit, and he ate it.*

There were two trees in the Garden paradise: The Tree of Life and the tree of the knowledge of good and evil. Whatever we eat becomes part of who we are. At first, Adam and Eve knew only God. And He is truly "good."

When they ate of the wrong tree, they partook of a source that included evil *and* good. However, it was a false good that only looked good on the surface. We can easily recognize many tricksters in the world today. However, there are many things that appear to be "good" but they're not the God kind of good. They spring from the *false good* that only appears to be good.

Instead of one source, God, ruling over everything and bringing forth the true good, an evil source began to wage war for control. The snake, satan, that old con artist, deceived Eve by pretending to offer something good. Most people resist things that are obviously evil but get sucked in by phony good.

God is really smart. He sent His Son, Jesus, to bring an end to the war. Oh it's not over yet, but God wrote the finale in His book, the Bible. So, we enter into what God is doing and become part of the mop up crew.

But we can't be on Team Jesus while we are still pawns of the "fakester," satan. Have you ever seen in real life or in a video a football player become confused and run the ball in the wrong way, even making a goal for the opposing team? That's what we do when we're fooled into thinking false good is God's good. How can we tell which is which?

Fortunately, Jesus, who is the Tree of Life, has provided us with a way to tell. We can assess the source by the fruit produced!

*A good tree cannot bear bad fruit, nor can a bad tree bear good fruit* (Matthew 7:20).

Socialism has seemed like a good idea to many individuals throughout the centuries. The purpose of this book is to provide a strategy for inspecting fruit. Remember, Jesus Himself tells us to verify good and evil according to His standards. Jesus rebuked religious people in Israel, the Pharisees, who *thought* they were doing good by telling them that the *source* of fruit is all-important. Is the source our Heavenly Father or the father of lies? All "good" apart from God is not God's good.

*You belong to your father, satan, and you want to carry out your father's desires. From the start he was a murderer, and he has never stood by the truth, because there is no truth in him. When he tells a lie, he is speaking in character; because he is a liar—indeed, the inventor of the lie!* (John 4:8 CJB).

What does Jesus want for us? Good fruit or bad fruit? And what does satan have planned for us? Good fruit or bad fruit?

Jesus bottom-lines it here:

*The thief's purpose is to steal and kill and destroy. My purpose is to give them a rich and satisfying life* (John 10:10 NLT).

Ultimately, fruit is produced over the long-term so we must both look back into the past and gaze forward into the future. What has the fruit been in the past, what fruit is being produced now, and what will be the eventual harvest?

We encourage you to start inspecting fruit!

# CHAPTER 1

# TOO CLOSE FOR COMFORT

Some ideas sound inspiring and even look good on paper but don't work well in real life. For example, suppose a man spent a lifetime studying birds in flight. He comes to believe that the key to flight lies in the motion of the wings. Other animals, he reasons, don't fly because they don't move their front legs or arms the right way.

After years of studying, drawing, and making calculations, he begins practicing. Day after day he spends hours flapping his arms like bird wings. Finally, he is ready to climb up on the roof of a high building to test his theory. Would you advise him to jump? After all, he is very sincere. He believes that he has all the facts. However, he is *sincerely wrong*! In practice, his theory would fail miserably, perhaps with deadly consequences.

What about socialism? Or communism for that matter?

Many people who have never experienced it personally think that socialism/communism sounds like a good idea. Ronald Reagan once said, "How can you tell a Communist? Well, it's someone who reads Marx and Lenin. How can you tell an anti-Communist? It's someone who understands Marx and Lenin."

It's one thing to philosophize about something and another thing for it to appear on your doorstep. Let's imagine how the concept of socialism might actually play out close to home to understand it better. Close to *your* home in fact. What would happen if *your* neighborhood formed a socialist government? What if socialism came a little too close for comfort?

---

What would happen if your neighborhood formed a socialist government?

---

## A Socialist/Communist Neighborhood

Suppose that your neighborhood Home Owners Association (HOA) says it is not fair for some neighbors to have more than others. They tell you that you have been treated unfairly and deserve more. They point out that some neighbors live in mansions, but most live in much smaller houses.

You begin to be envious of your richer neighbors and want what they have. The HOA promises you that if they were in charge, they would take from the rich to give you everything you need. They promise to right the economic wrongs. "It's all about equality," the HOA exclaims.

Wait! What vital point are you missing here? Aren't you even slightly skeptical about the claims made by television commercials or car salesmen? You know that they are not looking out for your best interests, they just want to sell you something.

When individuals are promised better housing, great retirement benefits, never-ending unemployment benefits, free healthcare, free college, a living wage, and all other entitlements from the government, it is truly astounding that people actually believe the politicians are really looking out for them. Look at the riots in Greece and England back in 2011. Governments were going broke, they couldn't keep their promises, and the people rioted to demand the entitlements to which they had grown accustomed. Governments couldn't keep their promises because they ran out of the taxpayers' money.

As Margaret Thatcher once pointed out, "Socialist governments...always run out of other people's money."[1]

Socialist governments always run
out of other people's money!

Question! Question their motives. Question their honesty. Remember that the words "crooked" and "politician" are paired together for a reason. Start asking, "Why?" Why are they promising you this? Are they *really* concerned about you? Are they truly so altruistic, so compassionate, so generous that they are only thinking about your welfare? Or do they have a *hidden agenda* you are overlooking? Is there a possibility that you are being... conned?

Now, back to the neighborhood:

- You give up your rights and freedoms and grant the HOA power to control the neighborhood economy. You vote them into POWER to "right the wrongs!"

- "From each according to ability, to each according to need," the HOA says. Everyone thinks, "I'll get all I need!" and imagines living in a wonderful utopia.

- Everyone gives their money and property to the HOA so they can redistribute the wealth of the neighborhood in a more equitable way.

- The HOA, however, takes most of the money to run the government, pay their employees, and make sure they get big paychecks and really nice vacations. And they themselves move into the nicest houses after evicting the original owners. After all, "everyone is equal but some are more equal than others!" (*Animal Farm*, by George Orwell.)

- The HOA decides your house is too big for just your family, so they move in four more families.

- You still get the same as your neighbors, even if you work harder; so everyone cuts back and less is produced.

- Rationing begins.

- The HOA decides you are using too much electricity, so they only allow you to turn on the lights for two hours a day.

- The HOA decides that individuals older than sixty-five are too old to do enough work and are using up resources that could benefit more productive neighbors in the collective.

- So, for the good of the neighborhood, the HOA comes to the conclusion that the elderly must be euthanized.

*Does that seem shocking? Read this quote by a famous socialist.*

George Bernard Shaw (1856-1950), Irish playwright, co-founder of the London School of Economics, and Fabian Socialist, stated:

> The moment we face it frankly, we are driven to the conclusion that the community has a right to put a price on the right to live in it. ...If people are fit to live, let them live under decent human conditions. If they are not fit to live, kill them in a decent human way. Is it any wonder that some of us are driven to prescribe the lethal chamber as the solution for the hard cases which are at present made the excuse for dragging all the other cases down to their level, and the only solution that will create a sense of full social responsibility in modern populations?[2]

The lie is that you can get something for nothing. Too many people believe the Big Lie without questioning it for three main reasons:

First, people get hooked by their own greed. If two small children are asked to choose between two pieces of unevenly sliced cake, each will invariably want the larger slice. It is just human nature to be greedy.

Advertising campaigns use greed and lust to sell cars. A commercial shows a person pulling up with a nice new Brand X car, with all the neighbors looking at it enviously. This is manipulation.

The marketers are appealing to your baser appetites, not your higher nature. Politicians use the tool of *class envy*. They deliberately stir up greed by pointing out certain groups of people who have more than others. The politicians then promise to "take from the rich to give to the poor."

---

## The Big Lie: "You can get something for nothing."

---

This manipulative strategy was used by President Franklin D. Roosevelt to get Americans to agree to the income tax. The 1935 Act was popularly known at the time as the "Soak the Rich" tax. Did the income tax really soak just the rich, or did it soak everyone, including you? That's how they trick the people. Who gets to spend the money? The politicians! Ironically, charities have to work much harder than politicians because moving people to feel *compassion* is much more difficult than causing them to *sin*.

Secondly, some people are lazy and like the idea of living off others so they don't have to work. Would you voluntarily cut your own grass if you thought someone else would do it *for* you? Would children voluntarily clean their own room if mom always did it for them? Probably not! It is just human nature to be irresponsible.

Parents have to *teach* a child to have a good work ethic. It doesn't come naturally. Do children become more grateful, or more demanding when they become dependent? Would they treat their mother with respect if she became a slave to their every whim, or would they become domineering dictators?

Benjamin Franklin (1706-1790) had observed first-hand the destructive effects of socialism and welfare dependency in England. He said it created people who are "idle, dissolute, drunken, and insolent," and took from them "all inducements to industry, frugality, and sobriety."

> I am for doing good to the poor, but I differ in opinion of the means. I think the best way of doing good to the poor, is not making them easy in poverty, but leading or driving them out of it. In my youth I travelled much, and I observed in different countries, that the more public provisions were made for the poor, the less they provided for themselves, and of

course became poorer. And, on the contrary, the less was done for them, the more they did for themselves, and became richer.

—Benjamin Franklin, London Chronicle, November 29, 1766

Finally, some individuals really believe the ideology of socialism/communism is fair and noble. These idealists, however, seldom study the historical evidence to see if it has ever worked. Failing to truly understand human nature, they envision only the beauty of the ideal. They fantasize, "Wouldn't it be just wonderful if people would just get along, share everything with everyone else, be compliant workers for the collective, and do everything their leaders tell them to do?"

Wow! That sounds a lot like how parents dream about home life and their children. "Wouldn't it be lovely if everyone would just stop fighting, stop wanting their own way, and our teenagers would do what they are told?" Yes, it certainly would be wonderful. What a lovely fantasy! Then everyone would be just like Mother Theresa! However, it is just human nature to be selfish and rebellious. Nice dream, but not very likely. People are *not* angels. James Madison, the Father of the Constitution, said:

> If men were angels, no government would be necessary. If angels were to govern men,

neither external nor internal controls on government would be necessary.

—*The Federalist 51*, Independent
Journal, February 6, 1778

The socialists/communists believe several things that are fundamentally wrong. They actually believe that man is good and civilization makes man bad. Therefore, if they can restructure society, man's goodness can emerge. However, our Founding Fathers had no delusions about the sinful bent of the human heart.

---

If men were angels, no government
would be necessary.

---

They understood that men are *not* angels. Citizens making up the general population must be governed by law and the individuals in power must be restrained or they will become tyrants. The Founders knew that human beings are sinners and they become greedy for wealth and power.

Socialists and communists are convinced they alone are the enlightened ones who must construct the ideal society through social engineering, because ordinary people are too stupid to construct this utopia by themselves. They divide mankind into two classes: the ruling elite and the stupid herd. They view themselves as the wise ranchers and the ignorant citizens as a herd of cattle they must control.[3, 4]

The Founding Fathers of America respected human beings because they are created in the image of God even though they were flawed by sin. The Founders believed that God gave men rights and civil government should protect those rights. America's Founders believed that a people who lived in humility under the rule of God and His precepts could govern their own lives and then govern the government. This was the great American experiment. "Can man govern himself?"

---

The great American experiment:
"Can man govern himself?"

---

## The Terrible Truth: You Trade Your Freedom for *Slavery!*

What would a ruling elite possibly get out of having power to control the wealth?

Power and wealth for *themselves*, of course! Even if they sincerely believe in the ideology, do you honestly think they *really* care about individuals? The truth is that they want to make you so afraid to lose your entitlements that you will keep voting them into office! They promise you things, and you become part of their voting base. If you don't vote for them, you lose your benefits. Even if they supply less and less, they still rule you through fear. It is a trap. You become their...slave!

Fear is the foundation of most governments.
—JOHN ADAMS, *Thoughts*
*on Government*, 1776

## Good News of Freedom

Jesus came to set the captives free. He proclaimed the good news of freedom to all mankind. Why should we allow ourselves to become enslaved to any man or government when Jesus came to set us free from slavery? However, it is important to realize that Jesus came not to set us free *from* civil government, but to reveal His freedom formula *for* godly civil government. When Jesus stood in the synagogue at the beginning of His ministry, He read from Isaiah 61:1-2, proclaiming the heart of who Jesus is, and His mission for mankind as the anointed One, the Christ.

> *The Spirit of the Lord is upon Me,*
> *Because He has anointed Me*
> *To preach the gospel to the poor;*
> *He has sent Me to heal the brokenhearted,*
> *To proclaim liberty to the captives*
> *And recovery of sight to the blind,*
> *To set at liberty those who are oppressed;*
> *To proclaim the acceptable year of the Lord*
> (Luke 4:18).

How many people think of "liberty to the captives" and "liberty for the oppressed" as individual salvation? Is there a "collective salvation"? Not in the same way taught by communist liberation theology, which is just another flavor of Marxism. Collective salvation has nothing to do with faith, or Christ, or spiritual salvation. It just means forming a socialist or communist "collective" community or nation for forced income equality.

God is indeed concerned about nations as well as individual salvation, but His ideas are vastly different from communism. God promised His Son the nations of the earth.

> *I will declare the decree:*
> *The Lord has said to Me,*
> *"You are My Son,*
> *Today I have begotten You.*
> *Ask of Me, and I will give You*
> *The nations for Your inheritance,*
> *And the ends of the earth for Your possession"*
> (Psalm 2:7-9).

The day will come when entire nations will be judged by God as goat or sheep nations based on their response to God.

> *When the Son of Man comes in His glory, and*
> *all the holy angels with Him, then He will sit on*

*the throne of His glory. All the nations will be
gathered before Him, and He will separate them
one from another, as a shepherd divides his sheep
from the goats* (Matthew 25:31-32).

In Isaiah 9:6-7, we are told that Jesus will bring His
government and peace to the earth and He will order and
establish His kingdom with judgment and justice:

*For unto us a Child is born,
Unto us a Son is given;
And the government will be upon His shoulder.
And His name will be called
Wonderful, Counselor, Mighty God,
Everlasting Father, Prince of Peace.
Of the increase of His government and peace
There will be no end.*

These verses are not talking about someday in heaven or
during the thousand-year Millennial Reign of Christ, but
the Lord actually governing on earth in the nations. Has
this ever happened in a whole nation before? Yes, twice.
God ruled in the nation of Israel and God established civil
government in America. America was dedicated to God
by the French Huguenots (1565 at Fort Caroline, Florida)
to become a dwelling place for God (Psalm 132:1-5).

In 1620, the Pilgrims at Plymouth, Massachusetts,
made a covenant and established civil government under

God through the Mayflower Compact. Both the Pilgrims and Founding Fathers of America acknowledged this holy calling.

> The general principles on which the fathers achieved independence were the general principles of Christianity. I will avow that I then believed, and now believe, that those general principles of Christianity are as eternal and immutable as the existence and attributes of God.
>
> —JOHN ADAMS, letter to Thomas Jefferson, June 28, 1813

> The highest glory of the American Revolution was this: it connected, in one indissoluble bond, the principles of civil government with the principles of Christianity.
>
> —JOHN QUINCY ADAMS

Jesus concluded His mission statement by announcing that He was ushering in the age of Jubilee for all people, "the acceptable year of the Lord." During the Year of Jubilee, once every fifty years, all Israelites who had sold themselves into slavery were set free, and all land that had been sold reverted to its original owner. However, Jesus came to bring Jubilee, freedom, to all mankind. God is the author of freedom. He proclaimed liberty through His Son and breathed the desire for freedom into the hearts of men everywhere—a God-initiated "yearning to be free."

America's Founding Fathers were architects
of a brand new form of government.

## The Political Spectrum

In modern America, politicians often talk about the left
and right sides of a political spectrum. The left ranges
from liberals to socialists to communists at the farthest
left. Conservatives are placed on the right side of the
scale, with Nazis at the farthest right of the right wing.
However, this doesn't make any sense, because Nazis
(National *Socialists*) were actually just a slightly different flavor of communist. What, then, is in the center?
Halfway between two forms of totalitarianism? And how
can those who love freedom be on the same side of the
scale as a dictatorship?

**AMERICAN POLITICAL SCALE**

Far Left        Center        Far Right

**Communist
Tyranny**
                              **Fascist
Tyranny**

## "People's Law"

Excessive government is tyranny. Too little government results in anarchy. Tyranny and anarchy are true opposites. Anarchy never lasts long, because the people begin crying out for protection and stability. And a tyrant inevitably arises to take control. Following the French Revolution, the nation devolved into chaos. Within ten years, Napoleon became emperor. France swung from anarchy to tyranny again in a very short period of time.

Our Founding Fathers used a different, more accurate, scale. They judged politics and governments according to *freedom*. Tyranny was cruel and oppressive while anarchy was violent and unstable. One was *total* law, the other was *no* law. 100 percent law on one side and 0 percent law on the other. So true freedom would be somewhere between total law and no law.

The Founders were looking for the **balanced center,** where men could live in the most freedom possible, but society would still be ordered and stable without sliding into either tyranny or anarchy. Thomas Jefferson called this balanced center **People's Law**. You could think of the Founder's scale like a seesaw that is balanced so it doesn't tip toward either tyranny or anarchy.

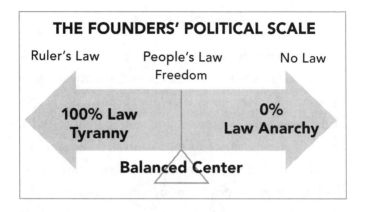

## Governing the Government

How could the governed actually *govern the government?* Was there a way for the people to elect representatives, live under the rule of law, preserve their rights and freedom, and prevent the government from seizing excessive power?

> The essence of Government is power; and power, lodged as it must be in human hands, will ever be liable to abuse.
>
> —James Madison, speech in the Virginia constitutional convention, December 2, 1829

> But what is government itself, but the greatest of all reflections on human nature? ...In framing a government which is to be administered by men over men, the great difficulty lies in this: you must first enable the government

to control the governed; and in the next place oblige it to control itself.

—JAMES MADISON, *The Federalist* No.51

The Declaration of Independence states that government must exercise power by the "consent of the governed." Government should not exert power over the people as in ruler's law. The U.S. Constitution, the Supreme Law of the Land in the United States of America, begins with these words: **WE THE PEOPLE**. What an amazing concept! Government works for us, we don't work for it. The government is our servant, and we are not its slaves. People's Law!

Governments are instituted among men, deriving their just powers from the consent of the governed.

—*Declaration of Independence*, July 4, 1776

Here sir, the people govern.

—ALEXANDER HAMILTON, speech, New York Ratifying Convention, June 17, 1788

## Discussion Questions

1. What is the "Big Lie" and why do people believe it?

2. What did James Madison mean by the statement: "If men were angels, no government would be necessary"?

3. The socialists and communists believe they can construct an ideal society. How do they view their role? What is their view of the common man?

4. Describe the Founding Fathers' beliefs about mankind.

5. Define "individual salvation" and "collective salvation." What is the difference between the two?

6. Is God concerned about nations?

7. What are the differences between the current American political scale and the Founders' Freedom Scale?

8. What is "Peoples' Law"? What is "the balanced center"?

9. What are the two extremes of law?

10. According to the Founding Fathers, what is the purpose of government?

# Endnotes

1. Margaret Thatcher. From an interview with journalist Llew Gardner for Thames television's *This Week* program on November 5, 1976. retrieved July 17, 2011 from http://www.margaretthatcher.org /speeches/ displaydocument.asp?docid=102953.

2. Edvins Snore, director, 2010, *The Soviet Story* [DVD]. Latvia: SIA Labvakar.

3. Gustave Le Bon, *The Crowd* (New York, NY: The Macmillan Company, 1925), 4-6.

4. Edward Bernays, *Propaganda* (Brooklyn, NY: IG Publishing, 2005, originally published 1928), 37-39.

# CHAPTER 2

# THE QUEST FOR FREEDOM

*Every spot of the Old World is overrun*
*with oppression. Freedom hath been hunted*
*round the globe. ...O! receive the fugitive and*
*prepare in time an asylum for mankind.*
—THOMAS PAINE, *Common Sense*, 1776

In 18th century America, freedom was an idea whose time had come!

When Jesus announced His mission statement in Israel, He included the words: *"To proclaim liberty to the captives... to set at liberty those who are oppressed"* (Luke 4:18-19). Over the centuries since then, these words spoken by Jesus had mostly been applied to the salvation of individuals. However, in a vast wilderness far away from Europe, a revolution was brewing.

Could a *nation* deliberately choose liberty?

## Could a nation deliberately choose liberty?

Early America was populated by individuals who longed for freedom and many who had been compelled to flee from persecution. These refugees left Europe behind for asylum in a new land. They found a place of refuge in the American colonies far across the Atlantic.

> The [Protestant] reformation was preceded by the discovery of America, as if the Almighty graciously meant to open a sanctuary to the persecuted in future years, when home should afford neither friendship nor safety.
>
> —Thomas Paine, *Common Sense*, 1776

The dream of a brand-new form of government filled their hearts. How could a nation enjoy the maximum amount of freedom without descending into anarchy and then back to tyranny? After all, the history of nations around the world had swung like a pendulum from anarchy to tyranny.

Since the 1600s, Christian clergymen in the colonies had preached liberty from the pulpits of America. Called the "black-robed regiment" because of the long black robes worn by members of the clergy, colonial ministers were not a literal regiment of soldiers, but influential clergymen promoting American independence. They encouraged the cause of the patriots and helped galvanize support among members of their congregations. Their pulpits thundered with the cry that Christ Himself is the Author of liberty.

On Sunday morning, Jan 21, 1776, pastor John Muhlenberg climbed into his pulpit in Woodstock, Virginia to preach. In his black clerical robe, the traditional dress of 18th century preachers, Muhlenberg preached from the third chapter of Ecclesiastes. He read how there is a time for all things. There's a time to be born and a time to die, a time to plant and a time to harvest. Then his voice began to rise as he said: "There's a time of war, and a time of peace. There is a time for all things, a time to preach and a time to pray. But there is also a time to fight, and that time has now come!"

Then he did something his congregation did not expect. He removed his clerical robe revealing a colonial officer's uniform beneath. Muhlenberg then stepped down from his pulpit and challenged the men of his congregation to join him in the fight for liberty.

Just a few days before, he had been commissioned by General George Washington to raise a regiment from the Woodstock area. As Muhlenberg walked down the aisle and out the door of his church, a drum began to roll outside. One by one, the men of Muhlenberg's congregation filed out of the [sanctuary] and volunteered to follow their courageous pastor.

Bidding farewell to their families, some three hundred men rode away from Woodstock, with Col. John Muhlenberg in the lead to form the 8th Virginia regiment. Muhlenberg led those men throughout the War of Independence.[1]

Civil leaders such as The Reverend Thomas Hooker of Hartford, Connecticut, experimented at town and state level with forms of free government based on the teachings of the Bible. The colonists proclaimed and wrote of liberty, the God-given rights of man, and the duties and purposes of government. Long before the Revolutionary War, the flame of independence burned in the hearts of Americans.

---

The flame of independence burned in the hearts of the American colonists.

---

No country on earth enjoyed full freedom or had a government that was under the authority of the people themselves. When the time was ripe, American patriots came together to birth a new nation in accordance with their convictions. Our Founding Father's staked everything they held dear, even life itself, on an experiment in freedom. Can man govern himself?

The American Founding Fathers not only longed for these blessings, but were uniquely qualified to be architects of a form of government that had never existed before. They were occupied in diverse occupations and endeavors as farmers, lawyers, professors, soldiers, and politicians, but they were all brilliant scholars, philosophers, and students of history.

> The Founders' goal was to revive...ancient principles [for freedom] which would allow the sunshine side of human nature to enjoy virtually unlimited freedom, while setting up appropriate safeguards to prevent the doleful shadow of human passion, greed, and lust for power from spreading a permanent dark ages across the face of the globe.[2]

During the Constitutional Convention of 1787-1788, South Carolina delegate Charles Pinckney said he was awed by the American accomplishment of creating a new and nobler form of government. He observed that all other governments owed their birth "to fraud, to force, or to accident."[3]

America was founded as a Christian nation. Although some historians have tried to claim otherwise, the record speaks for itself. In the years leading up to the founding, America experienced the First Great Awakening. It has been said that almost every man, woman, and child had heard the preaching of the great orator, George Whitfield, during that time. It was pointed out that a colonist could live their entire life without encountering a nonbeliever. The Awakening united Christian colonists in a common salvation experience, broke down state and denominational lines, created a national identity with a common cause, and made America truly "one nation under God."

Our Founding Fathers expressed their personal faith and the importance of Christianity in the founding of America. Fifty-three of the original 56 signers of the Declaration of Independence were devout Christians. In a speech to the Virginia Convention in March of 1776, Patrick Henry said, *There is a just God that presides over the destinies of the nations.* For America's Founding Fathers, Christianity was the only true religion. Of the 39 delegates who signed the U.S. Constitution, at least 37 were devout believers.

> As to Jesus of Nazareth, my opinion of whom
> you particularly desire, I think the system of

morals and His religion as He left them to us, the best the world ever saw or is likely to see.

—Benjamin Franklin, letter to Ezra Stiles, March 9, 1790.

The general principles on which the fathers achieved independence were the general principles of Christianity.

—John Adams, letter to Thomas Jefferson April 19, 1817

The Founders themselves said that the miracle of a free nation could not have happened without certain necessary and favorable conditions.

These circumstances combined to provide the cultural environment which virtually compelled them to take this dangerous and exciting new leap into the unknown. The miracle required a certain amount of isolation, a common set of basic beliefs, a universal sense of urgency because of a common threat, and a generous sprinkling of remarkable leaders, in each of the regions, who were willing to meet together and strive for a common goal. The presence of all of these ingredients is part of the "miracle" which became America.[4]

## Advancing Freedom

Thomas Jefferson, the principle author of the Declaration of Independence, was seeking the ideal balance of civil government so men could be free but not slide into tyranny or anarchy. No such government had ever been planned out like this. There was no blueprint to follow. It could not be copied; it could only be invented.

When Jefferson pored over history searching for examples of freedom in government, he found a type in ancient Israel. He studied the biblical account in Exodus in which Moses' father-in-law, Jethro, suggested a plan of government which Jefferson considered to be a form of People's Law (see Exodus 18:20-26).

As Jefferson searched the historical record, he found only one other clear example of *People's Law* in history, besides that of Moses in the book of Exodus. In the unlikely location of the British Isles, a small group of Anglo-Saxons devised a system of civil government very similar to the system that Jethro suggested to Moses. They even called the leader of a group of ten, who exercised certain legal responsibilities and authority, a "tythingman."

> A free government could not be copied; it could only be invented.

The Hebrews called the tenth of a person's income which was given as an offering to God the "tithe," or "tythe" in Middle English. How could principles from the Scriptures have been discovered by these tribes? Some scholars speculate that they were descendants of the Lost Tribes of Israel, who migrated north to Assyria and eventually reached the British Isles.

Jefferson understood that the basis of English common law had been established in the British Isles with the arrival of Anglo-Saxon tribes under the leadership of the tribal chiefs, Hengist and Horsa, in 450 AD. Common law is the ancient law of England based on the customs of society according to the negative golden rule—don't do unto others what you would not have them do unto you. Common law was recognized and enforced by the judgments and decrees of the courts. An innate sense of liberty was planted in English hearts.

The Norman conquest of the British Isles, led by William the Conqueror (1066-1087 AD), took place over a five-year period from 1066 AD to 1071 AD. The invaders replaced People's Law with Ruler's Law. Following the Norman Conquest, the British struggled for centuries to regain the freedom they had lost. The cause of liberty and the natural rights of people advanced with the granting of Magna Charta in 1215, a rudimentary Parliament in 1264, Petition of Rights in 1628, and English Bill of Rights in 1688. The struggle for liberty was long and often violent. Many of the oppressed, still longing for freedom, fled to the American colonies.

> The sacred rights of mankind are not to be rummaged for among old parchments or musty records. they are written, as with a sunbeam, in the whole volume of human nature, by the hand of the divinity itself, and can never be erased or obscured by mortal power.
>
> —ALEXANDER HAMILTON, *The Farmer Refuted*, February 5, 1775

Jefferson was convinced that the form of government being formed in the emerging America was a restoration of the sublime Anglo-Saxon principles of law. Now America was at the forefront in the quest for liberty.

## The Wealth of Nations

Another significant event occurred in 1776. *The Wealth of Nations*, by Adam Smith (1723-1790), was published. Freedom was paired with Smith's blueprint for a prosperous national economy based oncapitalism, which is also known as free enterprise.

For Smith, liberty was all-encompassing. Freedom meant freedom of speech and freedom of religion, freedom to earn a living, freedom from stifling taxes and trade restrictions, freedom from oppressive government regulations, and freedom to own and use property for new businesses and competitive inventions. Free enterprise means that people are free to try, free to buy, free to sell, and free to fail, then try again.

Smith wrote that prosperity requires only peace, low taxes, and a good system of justice—the rule of law. The principal theme of *The Wealth of Nations* is that a nation promotes its own wealth most advantageously through having a framework of laws leaving individuals free to pursue the healthy self-interest they have in their own economic success.

---

Two key events for America occurred in 1776: The Declaration of Independence was signed and The Wealth of Nations was published.

---

## The American Revolution

General George Washington was drafted to serve as the Commander in Chief of the Continental Army of the United States on June 15, 1775. The first challenge was even making a semblance of an army out of the motley assembly who had volunteered from the farmlands and backwoods of America. Fortunately, the Continental Army did have the advantage of learning to fight like the Indians.

The Revolutionary War lasted for eight long and difficult years. Because the Articles of Confederation, an agreement among the 13 original states that served as its first constitution, gave the Continental Congress no powers to tax or enforce, the only recourse left to them was to make requests to the states. During the entire war, the states stubbornly refused all pleadings to provide food, money, or arms for the army.

> This left the men on the battlefield, who were doing the bleeding and the dying, too few in number, too exposed to the freezing cold, with too few guns to share, too little clothing, too few tents and blankets to cover them, too few rounds of ammunition for fighting, and often too many fronts on which to fight with such meager miserable resources. ...But the Revolutionary War demonstrated what strong men and women will do for the cause of liberty.[5]

## A World Turned Upside Down

Despite such trials as sleeping without blankets and tents, fighting in the snow with no shoes, and enduring the terrible winters at Valley Forge, Pennsylvania and Morristown, New Jersey, the Colonial army finally prevailed against all odds.

The entire history of the Revolutionary War is filled with ample evidence that only the hand of God could have accomplished this great victory. Finally, on the heels of their worst defeat, Washington and his army prevailed at the Battle of Yorktown, Virginia. The British Army formally surrendered to General Washington on October 19, 1781. At the final sword ceremony where the British soldiers marched forward to hand over their weapons to General Washington, a band played the tune "The World Turned Upside Down." The world had indeed been turned upside down.

> We have it in our power to begin the world over again.
>
> —THOMAS PAINE, Appendix
> to *Common Sense*, 1776

In his pamphlet urging independence from Britain [Thomas] Paine got very excited about the prospects for the American colonists in forming "the noblest, purest constitution on the face of the earth." Not since the flood and Noah had the world been in a situation where it would have to remake itself in a new form. Whereas the flood experienced by Noah meant the death and destruction of most living things, the American revolution was the opportunity for the birth of a new political world in which individual liberty, limited government, and free markets would be able to flourish.[6]

Although the war had been won, the fledgling nation tottered on the brink of anarchy, the British army was waiting at the border eager to rush back in when the new government collapsed, and the new nation was facing economic disaster. The British refused to abandon their posts on the frontier fringes of America because they fully expected to come back in and take over after the American experiment failed. Thanks largely to the efforts of George Washington, a Constitutional Convention was called and the U.S. Constitution was finally ratified on June 22, 1788. The participants marveled at what had taken place. Washington wrote in a letter to his friend, the Marquis de Lafayette, on February 7, 1788:

> It appears to me, then, little short of a miracle, that the Delegates from so many different States (which States you know are also different from each other in their manners, circumstances, and prejudices) would unite in forming a system of national Government, so little liable to well founded objections.

James Madison expressed his amazement:

> The real wonder is that so many difficulties should have been surmounted. ...It is impossible for any man of candor to reflect on this circumstance without partaking of the astonishment. It is impossible for the man of pious

reflection not to perceive in it a finger of that Almighty hand which has been so frequently and signally extended to our relief in the critical stages of the revolution.

—*The Federalist Papers*: No. 37, January 11, 1788

## Freedom from Slavery

Our Founding Fathers were architects of a brand-new form of government: A nation of free individuals where the people would not be owned by the government, but would "govern" the government. We must remember that America's Founders had a vision for a nation based on freedom but they had inherited a flawed system in which slavery was a fact, and this they despised. Slavery was passed down to them from the British colonial period.

America's Founders did not create a government completely in harmony with their own convictions. The institution of slavery was in conflict with their ideals—*"We hold these truths to be self-evident, that all men are created equal."* —Preamble of the *Declaration of Independence.*

They agreed that slavery did not line up with the principles of the Declaration of Independence and said so on numerous occasions. Based on their certainty that slavery was wrong, they tried to get rid of it. They didn't succeed in every state but they did succeed in many states. In

1776 *every* state had slavery as an institution. By the early 1800's slavery had been abolished in eight states. This means we can look back on their achievement as a good, yet incomplete, foundation for our republic.

Many Founding Fathers never owned slaves at all. A number of Founders freed their slaves, including George Washington, John Dickinson, Caesar Rodney, William Livingston, George Wythe, John Randolph of Roanoke, and others. The great majority loathed the practice of slavery, considering it to be inconsistent with their Christian faith.

---

The Founders inherited a flawed system.

---

I can only say that there is not a man living who wishes more sincerely than I do, to see a plan adopted for the abolition of slavery.
— *George Washington*, Letter
to Robert Morris, 1786

[S]lavery is repugnant to the principles of Christianity.
—BENJAMIN RUSH, signer of the *Declaration of Independence*, January 1, 1794

During this period of time, it was widely believed that the best way to end slavery was to abolish the slave trade. It was to this end that William Wilberforce worked tirelessly for more than 20 years in Great Britain. Benjamin

Franklin joined him in his efforts. The slave trade was finally abolished in England in 1807 and, one year later, in America in 1808. Unfortunately, more still needed to be done. Slavery did not just come to end in spite of these victories. How could they free the slaves *already* here?

In spite of the freedoms declared in the Declaration, slavery was codified in the Constitution. The delegates felt obliged to make a compromise. The majority of the Framers of the Constitution wanted to end slavery, but believed that the very survival of the nation was at stake. Therefore, Provision 107 in Article I, Section 9, Clause 1 gave the states the right to continue to import slaves and bond servants for 20 years, giving the states time to stabilize economically. But it then gave the federal government the right to terminate importation of slaves after that time.

The Founders believed that this provision alone would end slavery. Unfortunately, the cotton gin was invented by Eli Whitney in 1793.

> Whitney (who died in 1825) could not have foreseen the ways in which his invention would change society for the worse. The most significant of these was the growth of slavery. While it was true that the cotton gin reduced the labor of removing seeds, it did not reduce the need for slaves to grow and pick the cotton.

In fact, the opposite occurred. Cotton growing became so profitable for the planters that it greatly increased their demand for both land and slave labor. In 1790 there were six slave states; in 1860 there were 15. From 1790 until Congress banned the importation of slaves from Africa in 1808, Southerners imported 80,000 Africans. By 1860 approximately one in three Southerners was a slave.[7]

---

### All men are created equal!

---

It would take other sons of liberty and a civil war to finally accomplish full freedom as proclaimed in the Declaration of Independence, that *all men are created equal.* Finally, John Quincy Adams, son of John Adams, worked with Abraham Lincoln to formulate the very plan that liberated the slaves following the Civil War. Slavery in America was abolished at last!

> [The Founding Fathers] universally considered it as a reproach fastened upon them by the unnatural step-mother country [Great Britain] and they saw that...slavery, in common with every other mode of oppression, was destined sooner or later to be banished from the earth.
>
> —John Quincy Adams, Oration, July 4, 1837

Freedom burst into bloom in the American colonies with the signing of the Declaration of Independence in 1776, the framing of the U.S. Constitution, ratified in 1789, replacing the Articles of Confederation, and an economic plan to finance the new world. An unprecedented form of government was born—a model of liberty before the eyes of the world.

> [The Founders] accomplished a revolution which has no parallel in the annals of human society. They reared the fabrics of governments which have no model on the face of the globe. They formed the design of a great Confederacy, which it is incumbent on their successors to improve and perpetuate.
>
> —James Madison, *The Federalist Papers,* No. 14, November 30, 1787

## Four Key Epochs of History

### 1. *Military Might (pre-history-300 AD)*

During the first epoch of history, the predominant force vying for control in the earth was military might. This was the time known for military leaders leading great conquering armies such as Alexander the Great, Genghis Khan, Cyrus the Great of Persia, and the Caesars of Rome. In the $2^{nd}$ century AD, four world empires formed and dominated the known world including Roman, Parthian,

Kushan, and Chinese. Barbarians overran the civilized empires bringing this epoch to an end.

## 2. Religion (300-1715 AD)

Religion shaped the known world during this time, spreading influence through evangelism (Christianity), exploration, and religious wars. Catholicism, Protestantism, and Islam struggled for control. Islam and Christianity warred over the control of the Holy Land and Europe. Constantine (227-337 AD), who was Roman emperor from 306-337 AD, became the first Christian emperor. He had a vision of the Cross of Christ on the battlefield, and subsequently helped develop the Edict of Milan, which protected Christians from persecution.

During this time, Catholicism also warred against Protestantism. Religious wars included the French Wars of Religion in the 16th century and the Thirty Years War in the early 17th century (German states, Scandinavia, Poland).

The Crusades (1095-1291) were military expeditions undertaken to deliver the Holy Land from Muslim tyranny and occupation and to prevent Muslim domination in Christian Europe. The Crusades have been assessed unfairly by many historians and scholars. Jihad, Islamic war, burst out of the Arabian peninsula around 624 AD and Islam began waging jihad with the intent of conquering the world.

They subjugated Christian North Africa and took over the formerly Christian Middle East after which they set their sights on Europe. Whenever they defeated the *kafir*, non-Muslims, they killed the men and old women, kidnapped the boys to be fighters, and captured the girls for sex slaves. In eastern Europe, Muslims enslaved millions of European Christian children in approximately 548 battles beginning in 700 AD and lasting for 400 years.

From approximately 1095-1291 AD, Crusaders struggled to stop the onslaught engulfing Europe. "Shocking as it may seem, love—not of the modern, sentimental variety, but a medieval, muscular one, characterized by Christian altruism, *agape*—was the primary driving force behind the crusades."[8] It is true that some Crusaders did some bad things, but the cause itself was noble. Note that the Crusades were fought as defensive battles to save church, homelands, wives, and children, from Muslim brutality. There were eight major Crusades fought from 1096-1270 AD. Jihad continues today.

> [I]f the Crusades had never been attempted at all, it is quite possible that the warriors of jihad would have overrun all of Europe, and the subsequent history of the world would have taken a drastically different turn. Instead, Europe experienced the High Middle Ages, the [Protestant] Reformation and the

Enlightenment, and the foundations of modern society were laid.[9]

"The crusaders, moved by love of God and their neighbor, renouncing wives, children, and earthly possessions, and adopting temporary poverty and chastity, were described as going into a voluntary exile."[10] Despite the popular depiction of crusaders as prototypical European imperialists cynically exploiting faith, recent scholarship has proven the opposite, that every crusader "risked his life, social status, and all his possessions when he took up the cross."[11]

## 3. Politics (1215–1900 AD)

From the time of the Magna Charta in 1215 AD, governments warred against one another. The great struggle within the British Isles was for the rights and freedom of individuals. The American colonies fought for and gained independence in the American Revolution, establishing a new form of government. The French rebelled against the ruling aristocracy in the French Revolution of 1789, but after slaughtering 16,000-40,000 of their own citizens in the Reign of Terror (1793-1794) and ten years of chaos, they reverted to tyranny under the rule of Emperor Napoleon.

## 4. *Economics (present day)*

The war being waged now is a war for economic control. Capitalism requires peace, rule of law, and a low level of government regulation. It is a system of minimal control and maximum opportunity to succeed. Will we remain free under capitalism or be enslaved under socialism/communism?

## Discussion Questions

1. Thomas Jefferson searched history for examples of People's Law. What two examples did he find?

2. What role might the Lost Tribes of Israel have played as far as civil government in the British Isles?

3. How could a history of freedom have impacted the struggle to regain freedom following the Norman Conquest?

4. How significant was the signing of The Declaration of Independence and publishing *The Wealth of Nations* occurred simultaneously?

5. Describe the four key epochs of history.

6. What is the battle we now face?

# Endnotes

1.  Dan Fisher, "The Black Robed Regiment: Preachers Who Fought," *Reclaiming America*, December 20, 2010; retrieved October 28, 2020 from http://reclaimamericaforchrist.org/2010/12/20/the-black-robed-regiment-preachers-who-fought/.

2.  W. Cleon Skousen, *The Making of America: Substance and Meaning of the Constitution*. (Albion, ID: National Center for Constitutional Studies, 7th edition, 2009. Originally published, 1985), 4.

3.  Jonathan Elliott, ed., *The Debates in the Several State Conventions on the Adoption of the Federal Constitution, Vol. 4* (Philadelphia, PA: Createspace, 2018), 177.

4.  Skousen, 5.

5.  Ibid., 70.

6.  "Tom Paine on the 'Birthday of a New World,'" Online Library of Liberty; retrieved October 23, 2020 from https://oll.libertyfund.org/quotes/381.

7.  "The Cotton Gin," Eli Whitney Museum and Workshop; retrieved July 23, 2009 from http://www.eliwhitney.org/new/museum/eli-whitney/cotton-gin

8.  Raymond Ibrahim, *Sword and Scimitar, Fourteen Centuries of War between Islam and the West* (New York, NY: Hachette Books, 2020), 130.

9.  Robert Spencer, *The History of Jihad from Muhammad to Isis* (Brentwood, TN: Post Hill Press, Bombardier Books, 2018), 170-171.

10. Jonathan Riley-Smith, *The Oxford Illustrated History of the Crusades*, (Oxford, UK: University Press, 2008), 32.

11. Jay Rubenstein, *The First Crusade: A Brief History with Documents* (Boston, MA: Bedford/St. Martins, 2015) 13.

# CHAPTER 3

# ECONOMICS IN A NUTSHELL

Nobel-winning economist Friedrich Hayek described capitalism as *spontaneous order*. He believed that "the prosperity of society was driven by creativity, entrepreneurship and innovation, which were possible only in a society with free markets."[1] A free market society allows individuals to better themselves by hard work and education. Because upward mobility is possible, nobody is locked into a class or economic position. A free economy makes it possible for individuals to move up to a higher social and economic position.

# Upward Mobility

## Capitalism: Teach a Man to Fish

- The poor can get an education and work hard.

- Many of the poor become part of the middle class.

- The middle class becomes larger and everyone benefits.

- Members of the middle class get more education and work hard.

- The middle class becomes richer.

- Some from the middle class become wealthy.

# The Purpose of Government

Government is necessary to maintain order in a civilized society, defend against personal and national attacks, and to protect the rights of individuals so that the creativity of the human spirit can be released in an atmosphere of freedom.

Law should provide (1) enough law to *protect* us, but (2) not enough law to *oppress* us.

Citizens *hire others* to protect them and perform certain tasks. You vote in a mayor and other officials into office to handle administrative duties and make sure the community runs smoothly. For example, you could stand outside your house all day to protect your home from intruders or fire. Or, you can pay taxes to support a police department and fire department hired by your town officials. Taxes are used for paying salaries and buying equipment necessary to do their jobs, such as police cars and guns, or fire trucks and hoses.

Government officials are, therefore, servants working for us—public *servants*. If the government decides to squander the money you pay them to take lavish vacations and so forth, they are wasting *your* money and should be voted out of office. They work for us; we don't work for them.

A government doesn't *produce* anything; it only spends. Government doesn't create wealth. It consumes wealth. It gets its money by (1) taking it from citizens through taxation, or (2) taking it from future generations by borrowing.

The Preamble of the U.S. Constitution tells us that the government works for "we the people." We pay them with our taxes to perform certain essential jobs for us. The main purpose of the US government is to protect our rights to life, liberty, and personal property, or "the pursuit of happiness." As part of protecting our life, government is charged with guarding the nation's borders and defending us from those who wish us harm.

The government uses the income generated by other people: You, your friends, family, co-workers, acquaintances, and fellow citizens. Absolutely everything the government gives you comes from real people, your neighbors. Disability payments? Neighbors. Food stamps? Neighbors. Medicaid? Neighbors. Unemployment? Neighbors. Many individuals who would feel guilty stealing directly from a friend's wallet, don't hesitate to get all they can from the government. People learn to "work the system" because of:

- Laziness (they don't want to work)
- Greed

## Misguided Compassion

Doing something based on misguided compasssion doesn't make it right. Suppose you have a house and one car. Your neighbors, the Smiths have a nicer house, two cars and no children. The Joneses, however, have a dilapidated house, no car, and five children.

You ask the Smiths to help out by giving the Joneses one of their cars but they refuse. After all, they had to work hard to earn the money to buy that extra car! However, their decision just doesn't seem fair to you so you can't get to sleep that night. Finally, you decide to take matters into your own hands.

- ***Redistribution of wealth.*** During the night you sneak over and hot wire one of their cars and take it to the Joneses house. But, the next day the Smiths call the police because their car has been stolen and you get arrested for breaking the law!

- ***Rule of law.*** Anything that is **wrong for an individual** to do, is **also wrong for a government**. Government is not exempt from the law! In this case, if you break the law you suffer the consequences. The rule of law implies equal justice for all. Every citizen is subject to the law and nobody, not even a king, is above the law. In 1215 AD in England, King John signed the Magna Carta placing himself under the rule of law.

Socialism is governmental theft. It's a crime.

## Socialism Explained by Grades

The grading system in college is based on a free enter-prise-like system. Each student expends time and effort to earn grade points. They get "paid" for their work in grade points. The sum total of points earned is a student's Grade Point Average (GPA). If socialism were applied, the higher achieving students would have points taken from them to give to other less intelligent or lazier students—a redistribution of wealth, so to speak. If all the grade points were equally divided up, A students would get Cs and F students would receive Cs, also. Everyone would be equal. However, the A and B students would stop trying so hard. A professor actually tried this experiment with his students, and the class average fell to D.

Why bother to work if you get little or no benefit from your time and labor?

## Freedom and Capitalism

Freedom includes freedom of speech, freedom of religion, freedom to earn a living, freedom from stifling taxes and trade restrictions, freedom from oppressive government regulations, and freedom to own and use property for houses, new businesses and competitive inventions. Free enterprise means that people are free to try, free to buy, free to sell, free to fail, and then to try again.

## *Freedom releases healthy self-interest*

Most of us want the best for ourselves and this desire is fundamental in the heart of man. When people are given the freedom to make a living under a system of just laws, they will cooperate with others for their individual good—and benefit society as a whole.

## *Freedom brings prosperity*

People are able to prosper when they are:

1. Not hindered by government or monopolies.
2. Free to do business or work in any way they choose.
3. Protected from exploitation by fair and just laws.

# Corrupt Capitalism

Unfortunately, when *enterprise* is no longer *free*, and business gets in cahoots with the government, a toxic brew of *crony capitalism* results. Crony capitalism is not capitalism at all. Favor is earned and manipulated by politics and mutual advantage.

A shared monopoly develops which grants unfair advantage to the favored few, bestows special privileges and tax concessions, and runs competitors out of business. Government collects taxes from *citizens* to give subsidies and make favorable loans to pet companies (such as Solyndra, the now defunct solar panel company). Crony capitalism harms both consumers and the general economy. It benefits *only* government and cronies. Any government that manipulates business for its own benefit is greedy and selfish.

> It was not bad theory alone that caused the [financial crisis of 2008]. A clutch of the top executives of our greatest banks joined with fly-by-night mortgage brokers and august agencies of the government in an unspoken conspiracy of fraud, with their own institutions among the ultimate victims. While the fraud was happening, it was winked at and even encouraged by nearly every relevant regulatory and political authority, with a few ineffectual exceptions. The ideology was essential to the deceptions that, had they appeared in their raw and rabid form, might have been resisted.[2]

> If, from the more wretched parts of the old world, we look at those which are in an advanced stage of improvement, we still find the greedy hand of government thrusting itself into every corner and crevice of industry, and grasping the spoil of the multitude. Invention is continually exercised, to furnish new pretenses for revenues and taxation. It watches

prosperity as its prey and permits none to escape without tribute.

—Thomas Paine, *Rights of Man*, 1791

## Profit Motive

Businessmen and women who want to make a profit aren't all greedy, although there are bad individuals in every arena of life. It is wrong to envy those who have earned their wealth. Wanting to take what they have from them is greedy and selfish. They have a *right* to their own property just like you have a right to yours.

Wealthy business owners are often major contributors to philanthropic causes. As a whole, they demonstrate concern for their fellow man. Ironically, those individuals who lean toward socialism give almost nothing for the benefit of others. Givers are charitable and care about those in need. Greedy takers don't actually care about helping others.

Individuals who believe they have a right to keep their own property are correct. They do have that right! A struggle over property rights led to the American revolution. Read the Declaration of Independence. Check out the reasons for rebelling against England listed there! The colonists were angry because the Brits were confiscating their property by "taxation without representation" and using their homes to quarter their troops. Imagine a bunch of soldiers barging into your home and staying for weeks or longer. They use your family's beds while you sleep on the floor, eat your food so you are left with only cheese and crackers, and confiscate your laptop. Pretty bad, huh?

So, who *is* greedy and selfish? Any person or government who wants to take the money or possessions belonging to someone else. Any government that uses force to confiscate the property of its citizens is greedy and selfish.

## Greedy Government

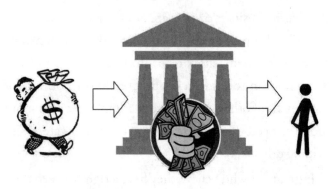

Government cannot create wealth. All it can do is consume wealth. We pay taxes and the government wastes our money. Ronald Reagan once said, "Government is not a solution to our problem; government is the problem."

Any government that uses coercion to confiscate the property of its citizens is greedy and selfish.

## Socialism: Give a Man a Fish

- Tax the rich and middle class to give to the government.
- The government is greedy.
- The government keeps most of the money for itself.
- The government gives some money for handouts.
- The poor use the handouts and then need more handouts.
- The economy gets worse.
- The middle class shrinks and the poor get poorer.

---

### Economics Explained by Cows

**CAPITALISM**

- You have two cows.
- You sell one, buy a bull and have a herd of cows.
- Your herd multiplies, you hire workers, and the economy grows.
- You sell the herd and retire on the income.

**SOCIALISM**

- You work hard and buy two cows.

---

- Your neighbor doesn't work because the government promised to give him a cow.
- The government takes one of your cows to give to your neighbor.
- You stop working, because what's the use anyway?

## COMMUNISM

- You have two cows.
- The government seizes both and provides milk.
- You wait in line for hours to get it.
- It is expensive and sour.
- Eventually there is no milk because of government incompetence.

## Discussion Questions

1. What is upward mobility?

2. Why is government our servant?

3. Why is something wrong for an individual also wrong for government?

4. Explain socialism by grades.

5. What is crony capitalism?

6. What are some purposes of government?

7. How does the government get money?

8. What is Adam Smith's prosperity formula?

9. Explain economics using cows.

## Endnotes

1. Linda Yueh, "Friedrich Hayek's Devotion to the Free Market," *Footnotes to Plato*; retrieved September 30 from https://www.the-tls.co.uk/articles/hayek-devotion-free -market/.
2. Andrew Redleaf and Richard Vigilante, *Panic: The Betrayal of Capitalism by Wall Street and Washington* (Minneapolis, MN: Richard Vigilante Books, 2010), 8.

# CHAPTER 4

# MAKING SENSE OF POLITICAL LINGO

*Socialism is a philosophy of failure, the creed of ignorance, and the gospel of envy; its inherent virtue is the equal sharing of misery.*
—Winston Churchill

To discuss capitalism, socialism, and communism, also called Marxism, adequately, certain terms thrown about in news media must be defined. Let's start with capitalism, or *free enterprise*. "Free enterprise, or the free market, refers to an economy where the market determines prices, products, and services rather than the government. Businesses and services are free of government control. Alternatively, free enterprise could refer to an ideological or legal system whereby commercial activities are primarily regulated through private measures."[1]

## Understanding Socialism

When asked to explain their understanding of the term "socialism," 17% of Americans define it as government ownership of the means of production, half the number who defined it this way in 1949 when Gallup first asked about Americans' views of the term. Americans today are most likely to define socialism as connoting equality for everyone, while others understand the term as meaning the provision of benefits and social services, a modified form of communism, or a conception of socialism as people being social and getting along with one another. About a quarter of Americans were not able to give an answer.

...The current research shows that Republicans are significantly more likely to view socialism as government ownership of the means of production than are Democrats and are more likely to describe socialism in derogatory terms. For their part, Democrats are modestly more likely to view socialism as government provision of services and benefits.[2]

Socialism has failed every time it has been tried. Yet, socialists persist in making excuses, saying that it just hasn't been tried the "right way." Capitalism, however, always leads to prosperity. There are countless examples of the success of capitalism, on the other hand. Perhaps we need to simply teach the truth so people can understand!

*Venezuelan socialism under Hugo Chavez.* Socialism is often presented at *getting benefits* from the government. Government produces nothing. Because government only has what it takes from its citizens, it has to acquire money through taxation or confiscation. The true nature of socialism is on full display today in both Venezuela and Cuba. As the old saying goes, a picture is worth a thousand words, so let's look at the plight of the Venezuelan people. Socialism was implemented slowly in Venezuela. It all began when Hugo Chavez, a communist, was elected president. Chavez didn't present himself as a communist or even a socialist. What he really believed became clear only gradually.

There [were] three main policies implemented by Chavez since 1999 that produced the current crisis: Widespread nationalization of private industry, currency and price controls, and the fiscally irresponsible expansion of welfare programs.

One of Chavez's first actions was to start nationalizing the agriculture sector, supposedly reducing poverty and inequality by taking from rich landowners to give to poor workers. From 1999 to 2016, his regime robbed more than 6 million hectares [an *hectares* is 10,000 square meters] of land from its rightful owners.

Nationalization destroyed production in affected industries because no government has the capacity to run thousands of businesses or the profit motive to run them efficiently. Instead, government officials face incentives to please voters by selling products at low prices and hiring more employees than necessary, even when that's the wrong industry decision.[3]

*Venezuelan socialism under Nicolas Maduro.* The policies of Hugo Chavez and continued under Nicolas Maduro have caused the ruin of a formerly wealthy nation.

Chavez died in 2013 and his successor, Nicolas Maduro, a former bus driver, doubled down on Chavismo. In 2018, 80 percent of the country was living below the poverty line and the annual rate of inflation reached 1 million percent, rendering the wealth of most Venezulan's nearly worthless. A study published by the United Nations...found that one out of every three people in Venezuela is unable to secure enough food to meet their daily basic dietary requirements. The assessment, conducted by the U.N.'s World Food Programme, found that 9.3 million people are "food insecure." Seventy percent of Venezuelans said that while food is available, they cannot afford it.

The economy imploded and the country has collapsed to the point that it is generating more refugees now than the Middle East, than Syria," said Niall Ferguson, a senior fellow at the Hoover Institution. In fact, in the last three years, 15 percent of the population of Venezuela has fled the country. "It's been a catastrophe and it's a catastrophe that was predictable if you understood what socialism does," concluded Ferguson. "I think it is important because so few people on the left in Europe and in the United States recognized Chavez for what he was.[4]

## Types of Socialism

*Pure socialism.* Communism is a "political and economic ideology that positions itself in opposition to... democracy and capitalism, advocating instead for a classless system in which the means of production are owned communally and private property is nonexistent or severely curtailed."[5] Pure socialism *is* communism.

*Democratic socialism.* The type of government in Germany under Adolph Hitler and in Venezuela now is *democratic socialism.* Democratic socialism has dictatorial leader who suppresses opposition. The government regiments society and controls industry and the economy while allowing some rights for the people such as voting in elections. However, elections are rigged of course. The one counting the votes determines the outcome.

*Identity Socialism.* Socialism requires a class of those who are oppressed pitted against oppressors. Socialism/communism requires manipulation, coercion, or deadly force to seize and keep power. Although the concept of socialism/communism can be traced back to ancient philosophers, Karl Marx (1818-1883) and Friedrich Engels (1820-1895) believed in the necessity of violent revolution to bring about revolutionary change.

If people are going to rebel, they must be recruited for "the cause." Their emotions have to be stirred up. Therefore, the instigators must give them motivation. They have to think of themselves as victims of oppression. In Marx's day, poor workers were the underdogs slaving under capitalist bosses. "Workers of the world, unite!"

However, in America, workers are now blue-collar middle-class individuals instead of the struggling poor. As a matter of fact, even our "poor" are wealthy compared to the poor in third world nations. It's hard to convince people that they are victims when they have houses, food, running water, indoor plumbing, cars, TVs, air conditioning, and good internet connections.

## Socialism requires a victim class.

So, who are the victims today? Enter the day of identity socialism! Socialism has been seen primarily in terms of an economic agenda. And it is true that some old-time socialist/communists still view the struggle in economic terms, but times have changed. Now the focus is on race, gender (feminists), indebtedness to student loans, and so forth. Anyone who sees themselves as downtrodden is a potential recruit. The movers and shakers of the socialist revolution of our day have discovered that they can energize erstwhile victims by utilizing cultural issues.

This is especially true of the socialists on campus. They are not in the workforce, so economic issues are distant to them. They are young and healthy—what do they care about retirement plans or Medicare for All? But they do care about their moral self-image, and they also care about their race, their gender and their sex organs. These are the identity socialists.[6]

Both Christians and Jews, are viewed as *oppressors* by those who hate God's commandments and whose mantra is tolerance. However, they want tolerance for themselves while refusing to be tolerant of those with differing viewpoints. Morality itself is seen as oppression. The white race has been vilified as upholders of Western Civilization and the Judeo-Christian ethic. These enemies of the socialist/communist sympathizers must be destroyed or, at least, marginalized!

---

Socialism requires a common enemy.

---

*Why do the nations rage, and the people plot a vain thing? The kings of the earth set themselves, and the rulers take counsel together, against the Lord and against His Anointed, saying, "Let us break their bonds in pieces and cast away their cords from us"* (Psalm 2:1-3).

Eager to distance their ship [of socialism] from earlier ones that have crashed into the reef, American socialists and leftists are trying to chart their own distinctive course. Even so, it's impossible to sail without some sort of a compass, so it's worth asking: What is the guiding model for American socialism? If it's not the socialisms of the past, is there a socialist system today that moves and inspires them? The unanimous response of the American left is, yes, there is.

That model, the progressive economist Paul Krugman insists, is not...Venezuela; it's Scandinavia. "Whenever you see someone invoking Venezuela as a reason not to consider progressive policy ideas," Krugman writes, "you know right away that the person in question is uninformed, dishonest or both." According to Krugman, Venezuela isn't really socialist. He wants us to ignore the insistence of Venezuela's former strongman Hugo Chavez that he was a socialist inspired by Marx and Castro.[7]

*Quasi-Socialism.* The idea of socialism has been growing in popularity in recent years, especially with the younger generations, and even among Christians. America does not have a fully free market system any more. This is because of government interference since the 1930s.

The common argument against socialism is that it simply does not work. It is an inefficient system that has destroyed societies and resulted in famine and death. This of course is true.

Socialism's impossibility results from its lack of a price system. In a free market, prices are subjective and determined by consumers. This results in the mutual exchange of goods and services by buyers and sellers. A socialist government attempts to set the prices of goods and services, but it is unable to set prices that will satisfy supply and demand (and thus socialist governments may look to the prices of capitalist societies). This is known as the socialist calculation problem, which was first introduced by economist Ludwig von Mises in 1920.

In contrast to socialism, quasi-socialism does "work" in a sense because it only ruins *part* of an economy. For example, the United States economy has been able to survive and even thrive with socialistic programs and a large welfare state. This is because there is still a free market in which businesses can function, and these businesses in turn fund socialistic programs. This is only possible because of increased societal wealth from improved technology and capital goods. In other words, quasi-socialism is only possible because of capitalism.

Furthermore, even the socialist industries of the United States have not been fully socialistic. For example, even with Medicare,

Medicaid, Obamacare, and heavy government regulations in healthcare, there are still cash-only doctors and private clinics that operate with some freedom. In spite of Social Security, many Americans still have private retirement accounts. And despite the ubiquity of public schools and universities, there are still many private schools and universities that compete for students.[8]

*Unification Socialism.* Scandinavia is a large region in northern Europe that is predominately located on the Scandinavian Peninsula. The Nordic, or Scandinavian nations include Denmark, Finland, Greenland, Iceland, Norway, and Sweden. Because the Scandinavian model is invoked so freely by the American left, John Stossel focused on one Scandinavian nation in particular, Sweden, in a recent article, "Sweden Isn't Socialist."[9]

According to Stossel, Sweden is not socialist. Not in the traditional sense anyway. There are plenty of entitlements but Sweden does not have a socialist planned economy. It has a capitalistic based market economy. Although Nordic-brand socialism works to a point, it can't be imported here. "We can't have Scandinavian socialism because we don't have the conditions for it. Our type of society doesn't permit it. Moreover—and this is the telling point—the American left doesn't want it."[10]

Sweden did have even more socialistic policies years ago but has now turned away from them by privatizing industries and repealing burdensome regulations. However, American leftists don't want Scandinavian socialism since they quite obviously prefer the Venezuelan form of tyranny if we look at their actions. Over the years, leftist politicians and celebrities have never visited any Nordic countries. However, they have been entertained many times by Fidel Castro in Cuba and Chavez and Maduro in Venezuela.

---

American leftists don't want
Scandinavian socialism.

---

Nordic nations have a unique bent *toward* socialism. It is called *unification socialism* and it seems to work for them.

> [Unification socialism is a] socialism of the tribe, and its distinguishing features tribal homogeneity and tribal solidarity. The whole point is to gather society into a single unit. The motto of unification socialism is that we are one people; we are in this together. The burdens of survival, and the fruits of prosperity, must be broadly shared by the whole society.

In the old Viking days, of course, Scandinavian solidarity was the product of the demands of survival in an extremely harsh climate. Viking tribes gained their booty in part through seafaring raids on other coastal peoples. They then shared it among themselves. The Vikings obviously had chiefs and ordinary raiders, but the key point is that the distance between the chiefs and the ordinary raider was much smaller than the distance between the Vikings as a group and everyone else. So...close identification...[preserved] the solidarity of the tribe.[11]

The people of the Nordic nations are much more homogeneous and willing to share than Americans could ever hope to be. But they pay a big price for their security. A celebrity recently filmed a documentary about the lives of ordinary citizens in Denmark. The interviewer seemed genuinely shocked to learn how little they needed to be content. Taxes are so high that most people live with few possessions in tiny box-like apartments with tiny closets. An interviewee smiled and explained, "We don't need a lot of furniture, a lot of clothes, and many pairs of shoes. We are happy without much."

A young college-aged man told us that he was shocked when he spent a semester in Denmark because the young people his age had no desire to be successful and improve their lives. It seemed like all initiative to better themselves has been programmed out of them.

## Suffering under Pure Socialism

### Venezuela

Amid Venezuela's political and economic upheaval, millions of children are facing hunger, preventable diseases, lack of education and violence. Chronic poverty and food shortages drive kids and their families to desperation, whether sifting through garbage for scraps or joining a gang—and facing brutal consequences.[12]

The western city of Maracaibo used to be Venezuela's affluent oil capital. But today, it's a place of hardship and hunger. Facing hyperinflation, corruption, penniless public services, crime and chronic shortages, the city has become a symbol of the country's wider economic collapse. Eating has become a luxury. Due to a lack of medical care, the lives of children, the elderly and those with chronic diseases are slowly slipping away.[13]

### Cuba

Behind Castro's revolutionary image was a lethal intent: he used his influence as an oppressor to persecute and punish those who engaged in dissent and opposed his dictatorship. Fundamental freedoms—particularly civil and political rights—were abused, and thousands of Cubans were imprisoned, beaten, and executed.

In the 1960s, the regime even went as far as profiting off of these executions by harvesting the blood of political prisoners prior to their execution. Roughly seven pints of blood were harvested from each prisoner, resulting in their state of paralysis. They were then lifted on stretchers, executed by firing squad, and buried in common graves. The Cuban government proceeded to sell their blood at $50/pint to Communist Vietnam.

Not even children were spared from the waves of arbitrary imprisonment and execution. According to Cuba Archives, at least 22 minors were killed by firing squad and 32 by extrajudicial killings under Castro's regime.

These horrific acts of exploitation and injustice are only glimpses into Castro's dark legacy.[14]

The draconian reality included acute food shortages, which led to outbreaks of malnutrition-related diseases, including one that causes blindness. The absence of medicine, including aspirin, meant turning to ancient herbal remedies for relief. The lack of gasoline meant that private automobiles virtually disappeared from the streets, and buses were rare and filled to capacity by people who sometimes waited for hours at the bus stop. Bicycles became the most common form of transportation. People learned how to stay clean without soap and to care for their teeth without toothpaste. They became accustomed to standing in line for hours for a meager ration of rice and beans. The kind of deprivation they experienced would have destroyed many societies, but Cuban society held together. Although the situation has improved since the worst days of the early 1990s, there are still chronic shortages of goods and the State continues to have trouble providing basic services like garbage collection.[15]

## North Korea

Even as people faced incredible hardship and deprivation of both the physical and mental variety and wasted away under food shortages, we weren't allowed to think for ourselves or take any initiative. The penalty for thinking was death. I can never forgive Kim Il-sung for taking away our right to think.

...It got so bad that we eventually started eating any old weeds we could find. We boiled the wretched things for ages to try to get rid of their harshness. But it was hopeless. They still tasted rank. ...No one thought or talked about anything except food. When we could manage to get around, we spent all our time searching and searching for anything remotely edible. We were nothing but a bunch of ravenous ghosts. The barely living dead. I don't know how many people starved to death. You heard stories all the time.

...The house in Hamju was dark because we had no electricity. There was no conversation between us. We were sitting slumped by the wall, staring out into the darkness. The moonlight was falling on my wife and children. Their bodies looked like trees in that chilly light. Dead trees. When you're starving to death, you lose all the fat from your lips and nose. Once your lips disappear, your teeth are bared all the time like a snarling dog. Your nose is reduced to a pair of nostrils. I wish desperately that I didn't know these things, but I do.[16]

Progressives, socialists, communists, Marxists, and American progressives all want the same thing—socialism/communism. They call themselves different names, but the goal is still the same. Most want to move slowly by small incremental steps through legislation and regulation. It's like putting a frog in water and gradually bringing it to a boil. The frog gets cooked but doesn't realize what is happening until it's too late.

The more radical members of the movement are committed to the use of violence to gain power, seize property, and force collectivization. However, the soft-speaking silver-tongued socialists all point to the Scandinavian countries as examples of a kinder, gentler socialism while craving Venezuela in their hearts.

Communism and Marxism are the same thing. Communism is the end goal of socialism. Communism is pure socialism. Three nations on earth have pure socialism today: Venezuela, Cuba, and North Korea. This is the utopian *reality* of socialism.

Communism is the end goal of socialism.

## Discussion Questions

1. What is democratic socialism?

2. What is identity socialism?

3. Explain Venezuelan socialism.

4. Explain unification socialism.

5. Why won't unification socialism work in America?

6. What is wrong with identity socialism?

7. What is the end goal of socialism?

## Endnotes

1. Caroline Cannon, "What Is Free Enterprise?" Investopedia, September 27, 2019; retrieved September 30, 2020 from https://www.investopedia.com/terms/f/free_enterprise .asp.

2. Frank Newport, "The Meaning of 'Socialism' to Americans Today," *Gallup*, October 4, 2018; retrieved September 30, 2020 from https://news.gallup.com/opinion/polling -matters/243362/meaning-socialism -americans-today .aspx.

3. Daniel Di Martino, "How Socialism Destroyed Venezuela," Economics 21, March 21, 2019; retrieved September 30, 2020 from https://economics21.org/how-socialism-destroyed-venezuela.

4. Matt London, "Venezuela: What Happens when Socialism Fails," *Fox News*, February 25, 2020; retrieved September 30, 2020 from https://www.foxnews.com/media/venezuela-what-happens-when-socialism-fails

5. James Chen, "Communism," Investopedia, September 29, 2020; retrieved September 30, 2020 from https://www .investopedia.com/terms/c/communism.asp.

6. Dinesh D'Souza, *The United States of Socialism: Who's Behind It. Why It's Evil. How to Stop It* (New York, NY: All Points Books, 2020), 25.

7. Ibid., 135.

8. Zachary Garis, "The Bible Prohibits Socialism," *Knowing Scripture*, October 1, 2019; retrieved December 7, 2020 from https://knowingscripture.com/articles/the-bible -prohibits-socialism.

9. John Stossel, "Sweden Isn't Socialist," *Creators*, January 2, 2019; retrieved September 8, 2020 from https://www .creators.com/read/john-stossel/01/19/sweden-isnt -socialist

10. D'Souza, 139.

11. Ibid., 140.

12. Marcia Biggs, "Sick and Starving Venezuelan Children Stoke Fear of a Lost Generation—and More Violence" *PBS*, February 21, 2020; retrieved October 24, 2020 from https://www.pbs.org/newshour/show/sick-and -starving-venezuelan-children-stoke-fear-of-a-lost -generation-and-more-violence.

13. Romeo Langlois and Jorge Benezra, "'We're Starving to Death: City of Maracaibo Symbolizes Venezuela's Collapse," *France 24*, April 24, 2020; retrieved October 26, 2020 from https://www.france24.com/en/ americas/20200417-we-re-starving-to-death-city-of -maracaibo-symbolises-venezuela-s-collapse.

14. "Cuba: 60 Years of Revolution, 60 Years of Oppression," *Human Rights Foundation*, June 18, 2020; retrieved October 26, 2020 from https://medium.com/ @Human_Rights_Foundation/cuba-60-years-of -revolution-60-years-of-oppression-99eedf90f7d2.

15. Catherine Moses, *Real Life in Castro's Cuba* (Lanham, MD: SR Books, 2000), 26.

16. Masaji Ishikawa, *A River in Darkness: One Man's Escape from North Korea* (Seattle, WA: AmazonCrossing, 2018), 55, 126-127.

# CHAPTER 5

# TEST BY HISTORY

Economics is the study of how people choose to use resources. It explains the production and consumption of goods, and the exchange and transfer of wealth for producing and obtaining goods. Economics describes the interaction of people within markets to get products or services they need or to accomplish particular goals. Since economics is a driving force of human interaction, studying it can reveal why people and governments behave in certain ways.

The two main types of economics are microeconomics and macroeconomics. Microeconomics refers to the actions of individuals and industries, such as the dynamics between buyers and sellers, borrowers and lenders. Macroeconomics analyzes the economic activity of a nation or the international marketplace. The history of macroeconomics reveals how economic theory and practice has changed from the ancient times to present day.

---

Economics is the study of how people use resources.

---

## History of Economics

Why study economics?

Economics is not primarily a collection of facts to be memorized, though there are plenty of important concepts to be learned. Instead, economics is better thought of as a collection of questions to be answered or puzzles to be worked out. Most important, economics provides the tools to work out those puzzles. ... Virtually every major problem facing the world today, from...world poverty, to the conflicts in Syria, Afghanistan, and Somalia, has an economic dimension. If you are going to be part of solving those problems, you need to be able to understand them. Economics is crucial.

...Economics seeks to solve the problem of scarcity, which is when human wants for goods and services exceed the available supply. A modern economy displays a division of labor, in which people earn income by specializing in what they produce and then use that income to purchase the products they need or want.

The division of labor allows individuals and firms to specialize and to produce more for several reasons: a) It allows the agents to focus on areas of advantage due to natural factors and skill levels; b) It encourages the agents to learn and invent; c) It allows agents to take advantage of economies of scale. Division and specialization of labor only work when individuals can purchase what they do not produce in markets. Learning about economics helps you understand the major problems facing the world today, prepares you to be a good citizen, and helps you become a well-rounded thinker.[1]

*Barter*. Bartering is the exchange of goods and services without the use of currency. Popularly used in ancient times, it has been a common method of exchange in societies or social situations marked by a low or non-existent money supply.

*Currency, coins and paper money*. Around 1200 BC, cowrie shells began to be used as a medium of exchange. Cowries are the most widely and longest used currency in history. From around 1000 BC, primitive coins were manufactured from base metals, and around 500 BC, coins were made from silver, bronze, and gold. In 806-1455 AD, paper currency began to be used in China, and was used in Europe after 1151 AD.

*Manorialism and feudalism.* The concepts of manorialism and feudalism (400-1400 AD) were prime influences on medieval European culture. Manorialism was an economic structure governing the management of land. It was mainly concerned with the peasants who provided labor on the land.

A manor consisted of a large main house for the lord of the manor, one or more villages, and up to several thousand surrounding acres. Manors, not villages, were the economic and social units of life in the early Middle Ages. Peasants were tied to the land under control of a lord. By 1000 AD, most peasants had become serfs, or semi-slaves, because of debt. Society was locked into a system that divided people into a wealthy aristocracy and a poverty-stricken underclass just like socialism/communism today.

> Feudalism was a social structure rooted in an exchange of land for military service. It was directed by the aristocracy, who were the landowners of the time. Land is the common element in both systems. Feudalism dictated how nobles gained it, while manorialism

mapped out how that land was maintained by peasants, the common people of the day.

...Land became the primary source of wealth in the Middle Ages. It provided the necessities of life as well as materials that could be sold for profit. One could not live the life of a nobleman without land. Indeed, one could not even fulfill his military duties without considerable income to pay for the expensive weaponry of a skilled warrior.[2]

Feudalism is a hierarchical system in which a lord or king gave a gift of land (known in Latin as a *feudum*) to a vassal, or knight, in exchange for protection. Since feudal Europe depended heavily on agriculture, wealth came from land. Land ownership became a way to improve social standing and become a member of the upper class.

According to the *Merriam-Webster online dictionary*: "In European feudalism, a fief was a source of income granted to a person (called a vassal) by his lord in exchange for his services. The fief usually consisted of land and the labor of peasants who were bound to cultivate it. The income it provided supported the vassal, who was obliged to fight for his lord as a knight."

Fiefs were granted to a vassal only for the lifetime of that vassal, but it is common for a son to inherit a father's title. This practice was called primogeniture. The decline of feudalism began during the time of the Crusades when a demand was put on the production of goods and a monetary system was developed.

> After the era of Viking, Magyar, and Muslim raids gradually subsided, Europe began to reorganize itself into a Feudal society. The old ways of the Germanic tribes were ending, which meant less freedom and more central power.
>
> The Feudal system was nothing more than creating a ruling class who owned all the land and wealth and provided security and safety to all the serfs; in turn the serfs provided work and servitude to their master. But many people do not realize the collective aspect of how serfs lived together.
>
> After the ruling class reaped the finest of the crops and livestock for themselves, the serfs were to distribute all the yield of their labor amongst everyone equally. They had no rights to any crops or land for themselves, all belonged to the community. They also shared in utilities. Most peasant societies had a communal oven[3] that was also shared to save on resources.[4]

*Mercantilism.* Mercantilism (1600 AD–1800 AD) was an economic system in which government control of foreign trade was considered of utmost importance to ensure the prosperity and security of a nation. It was based on the accumulation of gold, gaining colonies, maintaining a merchant marine, as well as developing industry and mining for a favorable balance of trade. Wealth could only be accumulated, not created.

Mercantilism dominated Western Europe from the 17th through the late 18th centuries. Mercantilism was a cause of frequent European wars during that time. It was also a motive for colonial expansion.

Feudalism and mercantilism were different in several ways. In the feudal system land and agriculture were the main sources of wealth. Under mercantilism, commerce quickly caught up with agriculture as the source of wealth.

...Leading up to the 18th century, the feudal organization of agriculture and trade gave way to a more capitalist organization of agriculture and trade. Political changes and the rise of the nation state marked the transition from feudal to capitalist economic organization.

*Capitalism.* Capitalism, or free enterprise, arose as a dominant economic force following the publication by Adam Smith of his five-volume book entitled *The Wealth of Nations* in 1776. He focused on the roles of self-interest and specialization to create wealth. Unlike feudalism and mercantilism, wealth was not based on acquisition of certain fixed resources but created wealth by unleashing human creativity. Therefore, wealth is unlimited. Capitalism frees people to act in their own self-interest by meeting the needs of others. No other politico-economic system in history has ever demonstrated its value so marvelously or benefited mankind so greatly.

*Socialism/communism.* Socialism, in a sense, is a step backward into feudalism. It promises equality but delivers an elite ruling class and an impoverished lower class. Socialism is based on a *false premise* that there is a certain fixed amount of wealth that must be redistributed for everyone to get an equitable share. Redistribution of wealth requires coerced taking from some to give to others. This is theft. Free enterprise is the *only* economic system that allows more wealth to be created rather than just moving around what people already have.

The three purely socialist nations in the world today, Cuba, Venezuela, and North Korea demonstrate socialism/communism in action. Those who escape from these nations do not want to return. Consider the words of North Korean defector, Yeonmi Park, (pronounced Yon-mee) who escaped when she was thirteen. In North Korea people were afraid to think because what they think might become something they say. If thoughts are expressed as unacceptable words and are reported, it might result in your imprisonment or execution. Her mother had warned her, "Even the mice and birds have ears." Now that she was free, Yeonmi wanted to study and learn. She developed an intense appetite for reading books.

> I read classics. ...I fell in love with Shakespeare. But it was discovering George *Orwell's Animal Farm*[5] that marked a real turning point for me. It was like finding a diamond in a mountain of sand. I felt as if Orwell knew where I was from and what I had been through. The animal farm was really North Korea, and he was describing my life. I saw my family in the animals—my grandmother, mother, father, and me, too. I was like one of the "new pigs" with no ideas. Reducing the horror of North Korea into a simple allegory erased its power over me. It helped set me free.[6]

---

Karl Marx: Socialism is merely a step on the way to communism.

---

## CAPITALISM

Why should it seem surprising that history repeats itself? Events may change but human nature does not. Both good and bad spring forth from the hearts of men: Deeds marked by cruelty, folly, depravity, heroism, altruism, nobility, and self-sacrifice. Let us now consider the history of free enterprise and socialism/communism.

## Ancient Israel

The scriptures gave the children of Israel very specific instructions concerning hard work, wealth, conducting business, economics, honesty, responsibility, and charity. Here are several principles found in the Word of God:

- God is your source (Proverbs 8:20-21)
- God owns all wealth (Psalm 24:1)
- Love God, not money (Deuteronomy 6:5)
- Give tithes to God (Malachi 3:7-9)
- Be charitable to others. (Leviticus 35:25)
- Work hard (Proverbs 12:14)
- Budget and save (Proverbs 30:25)
- Don't steal (Deuteronomy 5:19)
- Don't covet (Deuteronomy 5:21)
- Prosper financially (Psalm 35:27)

## Monasteries in the Dark and Early Middle Ages

The term "Dark Ages," now called Early Middle Age, was not merely a poetic name, but a very apt description of the immense loss Europe suffered when Roman law and order collapsed, giving way to times of great barbarity and uncertainty. As European civilization entered the Dark Ages, an era of intellectual darkness descended which was to last for some eight or nine hundred years. Even the ability to read and write was lost during this time. Only in the monasteries was a faint light of scholasticism kept burning.

---

The term "Dark Ages" was a description of the immense loss Europe suffered when Roman law and order collapsed.

---

Monks applied economic principles from the Bible to finance and commerce hundreds of years before the Protestant Reformation and the establishment of the American colonies. Although many historians have made the claim that free enterprise, or capitalism, originated in protestant America, in truth, monasteries during the Dark and early Middle Ages applied principles of biblical economics and prospered in a remarkable way. The roots of capitalism come directly from the Bible!

Although the individual monks took vows of poverty, the monasteries themselves became wealthy. Monasteries were landowners from the beginning because they purchased land and constructed buildings, but in the 10th century they began to accumulate substantial amounts of cash, land, and livestock, rivaling the wealthiest aristocrats.

A monastery provided local communities with spiritual guidance; very often its church was for wider public use, it gave employment, and its monks provided education, safe-guarded holy relics, entertained the pilgrims who came to visit, looked after orphans, the sick and aged, and daily gave out food, drink and alms to the poor. Monks produced and copied countless invaluable historical documents such as religious treatises, biographies...and regional histories.[7]

## Pilgrims at Plymouth, 1620

William Bradford, governor of the little Plymouth colony of Pilgrims, looked to the Bible for God's principles of economics. He studied the scriptures, then applied biblical financial principles based on the Word of God. The seed of free enterprise was sown in Plymouth, and the little colony began to be productive and thrive.

## One Nation Under God, 1776

The great American experiment of freedom commenced. The Declaration of Independence was signed in 1776 by 56 patriots who pledged their *lives*, their *fortunes*, and their *sacred honor* for the cause of liberty. As soon as they signed the document, all were instantly guilty of high treason against the British crown. They, in effect, signed their own death warrants. But from this courageous act, a new nation of freemen under God was born.

On April 18, 1775, a British soldier ordered John Adams, John Hancock, and other patriots to "disperse

in the name of George the Sovereign King of England."
Adams responded:

> We recognize no sovereign but God, and no
> king but Jesus!
>
> —JOHN ADAMS AND JOHN HANCOCK,
> April 18, 1775.

## The Wealth of Nations, 1776

Liberty in and of itself is magnificent!

> Liberty is the power to do everything that does
> not interfere with the rights of others: thus,
> the exercise of the natural rights of every indi-
> vidual has no limits save those that assure to
> other members of society the enjoyment of the
> same rights.
>
> —THOMAS PAINE, Plan of a
> Declaration of Rights, 1792

> Political freedom includes in it every other
> blessing. All the pleasures of riches, science,
> virtue, and even religion itself derive their
> value from liberty alone.
>
> —BENJAMIN RUSH, to Catharine
> Macaulay, January 18, 1769

Freedom allows people to think, plan, and dream.
But finances are required to fund dreams and ideas so
imagination can become reality. In 1776, Adam Smith

(1723-1790), Scottish social philosopher and a pioneer of political economy, laid out the economic theory of wealth creation in the first book of modern economics. His magnum opus, *The Wealth of Nations*, became one of the most influential works on economics ever written. Smith argued that healthy self-interest, free markets, and competition produce prosperity. When our Founding Fathers needed to create an economic system for America, they used Smith's revolutionary principles.

Capitalism rests upon the concept of meeting the needs of yourself and your family based on observing what your neighbor needs and providing or inventing it for him to buy. You and your neighbor both benefit. You see a need, meet that need, and, in this way, provide for yourself and your household.

How did this economic system work out in the new nation? The combination of liberty and free enterprise unleashed an explosion of human creativity that catapulted mankind from mule-drawn plows to the moon in 200 years. Human imagination is wonderful but, without finances, ideas must remain dreams rather than reality. A free people plus free enterprise in America unleashed an explosion of creativity in inventions that benefited the human race.

*Christian principles.* Adam Smith believed that the creation of wealth must be governed by the Second Great Commandment to love yourself and your neighbor and the Golden Rule, to treat others as you would like others to treat you. "*Do to others whatever you would like them to do to you. This is the essence of all that is taught in the law and the prophets*" (Matthew 7:12 NLT).

---

### Healthy self-interest benefits individuals and society as a whole.

---

*Healthy self-interest.* Men will gladly work for themselves and their families when they can profit from their own labor. This benefits individuals and society as a whole. Adam Smith wrote:

> It is not from the benevolence of the butcher, the brewer, or the baker that we expect our dinner, but from their regard to their own interest. We address ourselves, not to their humanity but to their self-love, and never talk to them of our own necessities but of their advantages. Nobody but a beggar chooses to depend chiefly upon the benevolence of his fellow-citizens.[8]

*Free market.* A free market operates by the law of supply and demand with limited government interference.

*The invisible hand.* Smith called competition the *invisible hand*, or force of self-regulation, eliminating the need for outside regulators. In the writings of Smith, it is clear that He sees the invisible hand as the hand of Providence, or God, directing the dealings of men.

> The invisible hand is a metaphor for the unseen forces that move the free market economy. Through individual self-interest and freedom of production as well as consumption, the best interest of society, as a whole, are fulfilled. The constant interplay of individual pressures on market supply and demand causes the natural movement of prices and the flow of trade. ...The invisible hand metaphor distills two critical ideas. First, voluntary trades in a free market produce unintentional and widespread benefits. Second, these benefits are greater than those of a regulated, planned economy.[9]

### American Prosperity

Following the American Revolution, the Founding Fathers designed an economic system based on the principles of free enterprise. The combination of freedom and finance soon made America the most prosperous nation on earth.

---

The combination of freedom and finance made America the most prosperous nation on earth.

---

*Large middle class.* Adam Smith pointed out that "a rising tide lifts all boats." The resultant increase of wealth in America lifted the economy of the entire nation and created a large middle class. In addition, all individuals had ample opportunity to raise their standing in society through achievement, so there was a general climate of optimism and confidence.

*Affluence and generosity.* In the American climate of prosperity and Christian values, charity and compassion abounded toward the less fortunate of society. It was widely considered to be a Christian duty to look out for one's fellowman. Affluence bred generosity.

## SOCIALISM/COMMUNISM

### The Folly of Intellect

Smart individuals can have foolish ideas! Human *intellect*, man's ability to reason, is not the same as *wisdom*. A man may have a brilliant intellect but still come up with ridiculous conclusions, which produce unwise actions. Thomas Sowell, in his excellent book, *Intellectuals and Society*, explains the difference between intelligence and intellect: intellect is intelligence without judgment and the opposite of wisdom is foolishness.[10]

> *The tree of life was also in the midst of the garden, and the tree of the knowledge of good and evil* (Genesis 2:9b).

*They did not honor and glorify Him as God. ...But instead they became futile and godless in their thinking [with vain imaginings, foolish reasoning and stupid speculations] and their senseless minds were darkened. Claiming to be wise, they became fools* (Romans 1:21-22 AMPC).

---

INTELLIGENCE = intellect + judgment
INTELLECT - judgment = foolishness
WISDOM = intellect + judgment + God

---

*For the LORD gives wisdom; From His mouth come knowledge and understanding; He stores up sound wisdom for the upright* (Proverbs 2:6-7).

*Go from the presence of a foolish and self-confident man, for you will not find knowledge on his lips. The Wisdom [godly Wisdom, which is comprehensive insight into the ways and purposes of God] of the prudent is to understand his way, but the folly of [self-confident] fools is to deceive* (Proverbs 14:7-8 AMPC).

Smart individuals can still have foolish ideas! We may assume that satan is smart. After all, he is a former archangel. However, in his pride, he came up with the ridiculous conclusion that he could ascend to the throne of God. It turned out to be a really bad idea!

> *How you are fallen from heaven,*
> *O Lucifer, son of the morning!*
> *How you are cut down to the ground,*
> *You who weakened the nations!*
> *For you have said in your heart:*
> *"I will ascend into heaven,*
> *I will exalt my throne above the stars of God;*
> *I will also sit on the mount of the congregation*
> *On the farthest sides of the north;*
> *I will ascend above the heights of the clouds,*
> *I will be like the Most High."*
> *Yet you shall be brought down to Sheol,*
> *To the lowest depths of the Pit* (Isaiah 14:12-15).
> *The Wisdom [godly Wisdom, which is compre-*
> *hensive insight into the ways and purposes of*
> *God] of the prudent is to understand his way,*
> *but the folly of [self-confident] fools is to deceive*
> (Proverbs 14:7-8 AMPC).

## Pagan Philosophers

Elements of socialism long predated Karl Marx and *The Communist Manifesto* of the late 19th century. The history of socialism can be traced back to Plato's philosophical work, *The Republic,* written around 380 BC. It is considered to be the philosophical "bible of socialism."

*Plato.* Plato (429-347 BC) was a classical Greek philosopher, born in Athens, Greece. In *The Republic,* he suggested that individuals were mere cells within the body politic, and the state should assign their work and responsibilities. Plato felt that the Philosopher class (of which he was one) should rule over the Warrior class, who would protect the state, and the Producer class who would serve the Philosopher class with manual labor, goods, services, and skills. The Producer class would be denied the benefits of schooling. Plato believed in communal property, as well as the communal sharing of wives. Children would be taken away from their parents and raised in foster homes supervised by the Philosopher class.

*Aristotle.* Aristotle (384–322 BC), student of Plato, criticized Plato's ideas in his work *Politics*, arguing that, without private property, no one would assume care of anything. If people had no property, they would even be unable to engage in social activities such as hosting guests or doing acts of charity, which encourage community and give meaning to life. Aristotle was wiser than Plato on this subject.

### The Enlightenment (17th-18th centuries)

During the Protestant Reformation a fresh wind of Christianity swept across Europe. As a result of opposition to Protestantism, many persecuted Christians fled to the American colonies, with a longing for freedom in their hearts. America was destined to be the birthplace of a government of freemen; the twin blessings of freedom in government paired with free enterprise were revealed to the world.

However, every time God moves, the enemy counter-attacks. Socialistic ideas swept through Europe during the French Enlightenment (1650-1800) and even negatively influenced the worldview of many intellectuals in predominately Christian America. However, America's Founding Fathers remained adamantly opposed to socialism.

---

Alexis de Tocqueville discovered an American nation which was unique in the world. Here, anyone could be a landowner.

---

Despite ample evidence to the contrary, many American intellectuals studying abroad became enamored with these European ideas that were opposed to everything America stood for. They were so deceived that they failed to comprehend the beauty of what God had created in America.

One *wise* intellectual, the Frenchman Alexis de Tocqueville (1805-1859), came to America and marveled. He was a political thinker and historian, best known today for his two-volume work, *Democracy in America* (1835 and 1840). Tocqueville has been widely cited for his praise of American democracy.

Tocqueville discovered an American nation which was unique in the world. Here, anyone could be a landowner, unlike European nations. He recognized the characteristics that made America great and set it apart from Europe. The goodness of the citizens, the righteousness preached from the pulpits, the Puritan work ethic, the thrift, virtue, charity, and generosity resulted in a prosperous Christian people. He called Americans a brand-new breed of man.

Yet, American intellectuals who succumbed to the seduction of the dark, destructive ideas of the Enlightenment were often unable to appreciate what was evident right before their eyes.

*Utopian mythology.* A utopia is an ideal society or community under a perfectly ordered social, economic, and political system. The word was coined by Sir Thomas More for his 1516 book, *Utopia*. Many philosophers and thinkers have toyed with utopian thought. Ironically, Jean-Jacques Rousseau (1712-1778), a Genevan utopian philosopher during the French Enlightenment, had a great influence on the French Revolution.

Two key concepts Rousseau promoted had a major impact on both European and American intellectual thought. First, Rousseau believed that man in his primitive state was pure and good, a noble savage. Secondly, he believed that civilization corrupted man. So, he thought, if civilization could be properly constructed, man's innate goodness could come forth. He described this ideal socialist society in his most influential work, *The Social Contract*, published in 1762. The group was everything and the individual was nothing.

Rousseau believed if citizens were *forced to obey* the *general will* of the community they would become truly free. Question: How can individuals possibly be *free* if they are *forced to obey*, or conform to, the will of the group?

---

How can individuals possibly be free if they are forced to obey the will of the group?

---

*Utopian socialists.* The Industrial Revolution was a chaotic time that wrenched nations from agrarian to industrial societies. Every time great change comes, great adjustment is necessary, but eventually life settles down and society advances. The excesses of poverty and inequality were widely lamented during the upheaval caused by the Industrial Revolution. The first modern socialists were early 19th century Western European social critics during a time of turmoil. During this period, socialism emerged out of a diverse array of doctrines and social experiments associated primarily with British and French thinkers—especially Robert Owen, Charles

Fourier, Pierre-Joseph Proudhon, Louis Blanc, and Saint-Simon.

The first use of the word *socialism* cannot be determined. It has been attributed to a number of people. Regardless of who actually coined the term, Robert Owen, a Welsh manufacturer, is considered the father of the cooperative movement in America. Owen (1771-1858) was a Welsh manufacturer who sponsored several experimental utopian communities of "Owenites" in England and America, including one at New Harmony, Indiana in 1825.

However, New Harmony soon disintegrated into *disharmony*. The community quickly fell apart, and Owen lamented that the Americans were "too individualistic" to be good socialists. Josiah Warren, one of the participants, later wrote, "It seemed that the difference of opinion, tastes and purposes increased just in proportion to the demand for conformity" (Periodical Letter II, 1856).[11]

The fatal flaw in Marx's philosophy was that it was based in lust for power and love of an ideology—not love for people.

Socialists tried to answer the problems of society by looking to human reasoning for solutions. They did not look to God, but their own intellects. *"Professing to be wise, they became fools"* (2 Thessalonians 3:9-10).

Unfortunately, even the churches in America during 1800-1890 became infected with lofty-sounding but impractical ideas of Christian socialism. Many based their attempts at communal living on scriptures such as Acts 4:32, *"they had all things in common."* However, they failed to understand that even good sounding ideas are foolishness apart from God.

> *For even when we were with you, we commanded you this: If anyone will not work, neither shall he eat. For we hear that there are some who walk among you in a disorderly manner, not work-ing at all, but are busybodies* (2 Thessalonians 3:9-10).

Americans are "too individualistic"
to be good socialists.

## Communism

**Karl Marx** (1818-1883) was a German philosopher, sociol-ogist, economic historian, journalist, and revolutionary socialist who, along with Friedrich Engels (1820-1825), developed the socio-political theory of Marxism. Marx despised the very idea of God. Although he had attended church as a child, he became a satanist and hated God! "He had the devil's view of the world, and the devil's malignity. Sometimes he seemed to know that he was accomplishing works of evil."[12] Marx never worked at a regular job, preferring to sponge off his father, mother, relatives, Engels, and others. His family lived in squalor and near poverty as a result.[13]

Marx believed that socialism would, in its turn, eventually be replaced by a stateless, classless society called pure communism. In addition to being fully convinced of the inevitability of socialism and communism, Marx believed in violent revolution to bring it about, arguing that both social theorists and underprivileged people should carry out organized revolutionary action for socioeconomic change.

In an interview with the *Chicago Tribune* on January 5, 1879, Marx was asked: "Well, then, to carry out the principles of socialism do its believers advocate assassination and bloodshed?" "No great movement has ever been inaugurated without bloodshed," Marx replied. A major shift had occurred. What had once been merely a utopian ideal soon turned deadly.

## Fatally Flawed

*Flawed economic theory.* The false assumption of Marx's economic theory, described in *Das Kapital*, was his notion that *labor*, the actual physical handling of the means, tools, and materials of production was the source of wealth.

If this were true, nations with much manual labor and little technology would be more prosperous than those with highly skilled workers and much technology. It is blatantly obvious that this assumption is completely false.

*Flawed philosophy*. Marx's philosophy was based in lust for power and love of an ideology—not love for people. How can you say you to want to *help* people and then *kill* them?

Christianity, on the other hand, is a religion based in love. *"God demonstrates His love toward us, in that while we were yet sinners, Christ died for us,"* (Romans 5:8). Jesus says that the greatest commandment is to love God with all our heart, and love our neighbor as we love ourselves. In Galatians 5:14, Paul tells us that *"all the law is fulfilled in one word, even in this: 'You shall love your neighbor as yourself.'"*

## The Industrial Revolution: Spinning History

Sometimes people see what they want to see while ignoring the truth. A well-known example is the tale of the Emperor's New Clothes. Some tailors said that they were making garments for the king, but only the elite would be able to see them. So, when the king was paraded down the street naked, everyone was afraid to say what they really saw. They couldn't admit the truth. Only a child spoke up and said, "But Mother, the emperor has no clothes!"

*Improving conditions.* What have you heard about conditions during the Industrial Revolution? You've probably read history books that portrayed it as a time of great evils. However, honest historians now verify that the alarmists of the day were *not fully accurate* in their assessment of the early Industrial Revolution. Many socialists/communists could not or would not admit Marx's theory was wrong, although the evidence was certainly there. Even during the time of the Industrial Revolution, after the initial upheaval, any objective observer could see that workers were better off.

Incomes began to rise, prices were lower, health conditions and diets improved, housing and working conditions were better. Industry paid more than agriculture, so wages increased. Life spans were lengthened and child mortality rates decreased, which did increase the numbers of the poor, because previously they would have been dead.

Perhaps the most important development, which proved all of Marx's theories *wrong,* was the emergence of a middle class, which could now afford goods and products previously available only to the wealthy. *The poor didn't get poorer just because the rich got richer.* The standard of living rose dramatically in all levels of society.

*Ignoring the Facts.* One British Marxist, Eduard Bernstein (1850-1932), the chosen successor to Marx and Engels, began to understand the truth.[14] He recorded that the standard of living was actually rising in a positive way even during the early Industrial Revolution. Bernstein observed that, contrary to Marx's theory, wages were increasing and prices dropping.

---

> During the Industrial Revolution, wealth was being created and life was better under capitalism.

---

In other words, wealth was being created and life was better under capitalism. This was all the evidence needed to demonstrate the fallacy of Marx's theories in his own lifetime. However, when the cause is more important than facts, the only recourse is willful denial, deception, and outright lies. Despite such convincing evidence to the contrary, ideology was more important to Marx than truth.

Socialists understand free enterprise leads to *prosperity* and socialism drives nations into *poverty* wherever it is implemented. They don't actually believe that socialism benefits people. What they really want is *power*.

## Discussion Questions

1.  Explain the statement, "matter itself is not evil, but the wind behind it is either good or evil depending on how it is used."

2. What are some forms of "wealth"?

3. Why is "creativity" included as wealth?

4. What is "economics"?

5. What form of macroeconomics was in play at the time of Colonial America?

6. Under mercantilism, why was it necessary for nations to have colonies to be prosperous?

7. In your opinion, which system of economics cited in this chapter would encourage human creativity the most? Why?

8. It has been taught that the free enterprise system began in America. When did free enterprise really begin?

9. What communities of Christians applied free enterprise principles and prospered during the so-called Dark Ages?

10. Adam Smith studied human nature and conditions under which prosperity occurred. Explain these principles and how they could benefit individuals and nations:

   - Healthy self-interest
   - Free markets

- The invisible hand

11. What does "a rising tide lifts all boats" mean?

12. What is intellect without judgment? Why?

13. What philosopher is credited with writing the "bible of socialism"?

14. When the Frenchman, Alexis de Tocqueville, came to America, what did he say about Americans?

15. Explain two serious flaws in the economic theory of Karl Marx.

16. What evidence did Marx ignore which proved his theory wrong during his own lifetime?

## Endnotes

1. "The Division and Specialization of Labor," *Lumen Learning*; retrieved October 23, 2020 from https://courses.lumenlearning.com/baycollege-introbusiness/chapter/reading-the-division-of-and-specialization-of-labor/

2. "Manorialism vs Feudalism" Study.com; retrieved October 22, 2020 from https://study.com/academy/lesson/manorialism-vs-feudalism.html.

3. Clifford R. Backman, *The Worlds of Medieval Europe* (New York, NY: Oxford University Press, 2014), 196-209.

4.  Michael Aaron Jones, "Socialism: The New Feudalism," *American Thinker*, May 25, 2010; retrieved October 14, 2020 from https://www.americanthinker.com/articles/2010/05/socialism_the_new_feudalism.html.

5.  George Orwell, *Animal Farm*, (New York, NY: Signet Classics, 1996).
    In the allegory *Animal Farm*, mistreated animals rid themselves of their human owners and take over the farm. They then set out to create a utopia with justice and equality. However, their "utopia" that begins with revolution against tyranny ends up as a totalitarian state just as horrible. At first, it was seen primarily as an attack against Stalinist Russia. Today it is clear that attacks against freedom have devastating consequences and applies to socialist and communist states today. Orwell's dark comedy masterpiece is just as razor-sharp as it was when penned in 1946.

6.  Yeonmi Park and Maryanne Vollers, *In Order to Live: A North Korean Girl's Journey to Freedom* (New York, NY: Penguin Books, 2015), 230-231.

7.  Mark Cartwright, "Medieval Monastery," *Ancient History Encyclopedia*, December 14, 2018; retrieved September 16, 2020 from https://www.ancient.eu/Medieval_Monastery/.

8.  Adam Smith (1776). *The Wealth of Nations, Volumes I-III* (New York, NY: Penguin Books, 1986), 14.

9.  Christina Majaski, "Invisible Hand Definition," Investopedia, July 23, 2020; retrieved October 1, 2020 from https://www.investopedia.com/terms/i/invisiblehand.asp.

10. Thomas Sowell, *Intellectuals and Society* (New York, NY: Basic Books, 2009), 1-9.

11. Ann Caldwell Butler, "Josiah Warren and the Sovereignty of the Individual," *The Journal of Libertarian Studies* 1980, Vol. IV, No. 4.

12. Robert Payne, *Marx: A Biography* (New York, NY: Simon & Schuster, 1968), 317.

13. Paul Kengor, *The Devil and Karl Marx: Communism's Long March of Death, Deception, and Infiltration* (Gastonia, NC: Tan Books, 2020), 78-85.

14. Eduard Bernstein, *Evolutionary Socialism: A Criticism and Affirmation* (New York, NY: Random House, 2019).

# CHAPTER 6

# TEST BY THE SPIRIT

Mammon is material wealth and worldly gain under an evil and corrupt influence, or false god. It is a term also used to describe greed, avarice, and the worship of wealth in biblical literature.

*God and mammon.* In Matthew 6:24, Jesus warned that individuals must make a choice between serving the evil spirit of mammon and the Spirit of God. Whatever or whoever you serve becomes your master.

> *No one can serve **two masters**; for either he will hate the one and love the other, or else he will be loyal to the one and despise the other. You cannot serve **God** and **mammon** (Matthew 6:24).*

Mammon is not just a concept. There is spiritual energy attached to it. An individual can either serve the spirit of mammon, or use wealth to serve God and lay up treasures in heaven. "*Lay up for yourselves treasures in heaven, where neither moth nor rust destroys and where thieves do not break in and steal*" (Matthew 6:19-20). And: "*Each one's work will become clear; for the Day will declare it, because it will be revealed by fire; and the fire will test each one's work, of what sort it is*" (1 Corinthians 3:13).

In the beginning, God spoke and the physical universe was created out of tiny particles of energy. Even what we perceive as solid or liquid matter is formed from atoms and molecules, which are made up of energy particles. Atoms and molecules are not evil. Coins and dollar bills are not evil. However, what man does with currency brings it under the authority of either God or Satan.

*A flow of purpose.* When an individual uses money, it is *joined to* the purposes of God or the devices of the enemy. Money is caught up into a *spiritual force* like a jet stream. It is conveyed into one kingdom or the other, and it becomes part of a river, or *flow*.

> *Your riches are corrupted* (James 5:2b).
>
> *Cornelius, your prayer has been heard, and your alms are remembered in the sight of God* (Acts 10:31).

Spirit always has *purpose* attached to it. Purpose has an eventual destination. God is building His kingdom, and the enemy is building his kingdom, which is intended to thwart the will of God and bring destruction to mankind.

> *They gave offerings of whatever they could— far more than they could afford!—plead- ing for the privilege of helping out in the relief of poor Christians. This was totally sponta- neous, entirely their own idea, and caught us completely off guard. What explains it was that they had first given themselves unreservedly to God and to us. The other* **giving simply flowed out of the purposes of God working in their lives** (2 Corinthians 8:4-7 MSG).

---

Money is caught up into a spiritual
force like a jet stream.

---

*The spirit of socialism.* Socialism is a murderous eco- nomic, social, political, and spiritual system originating from the Tree of the Knowledge. It is not just another idea, opinion, or ideology. It operates through the sin of greed, promising something for nothing as the bait. It encourages individuals to sin by breaking the eighth and tenth commandments against stealing and covetousness. As in the parable of the tares in Matthew 13:24-28, the poisonous spirit eventually reveals itself.

## Test the Spirits

The Scriptures tell us that we have a responsibility to test the spirits. Question the *source* and the *spirit* behind schools of thought, teachings, and philosophies. "*Beloved, do not believe every spirit, but test the spirits to see whether they are from God*" (1 John 4:1). When we consider what is actually *produced* by an economic philosophy, the spirit behind it is made manifest.

---

Test the spirits!

---

Everything that comes from God has His nature attached to it. It has an anointing upon it. It is holy and undefiled. Does it feel pure or sinful, clean or unclean? Is it consistent with the love nature of God? Does it come from the wisdom of God and release the righteousness of God, which is obedience to God's will?

> *For where envy and self-seeking exist, confusion and every evil thing are there. But the wisdom that is from above is first pure, then peaceable, gentle, willing to yield, full of mercy and good fruits* (James 3:16-17).

| Spirit of Capitalism | Spirit of Socialism/ Communism |
| --- | --- |
| Allows freedom | Denies freedom |
| Rewards success | Punishes success |
| Rewards hard work | Rewards laziness |
| Encourages creativity | Promotes mediocrity |
| Respects property | Steals property |
| Promotes charity | Promotes greed |
| Respects God-given rights<br>• Life<br>• Liberty<br>• Property | Violates God-given rights<br>• Life *(abortion, euthanasia)*<br>• Liberty *(political correctness,* control*)*<br>• Property (theft) |

# THE CHOICE: GOD OR MAMMON

When we become citizens of God's kingdom, we have spiritual authority to break the power of mammon over our money and bring it under God's control. "*He has delivered us from the power of darkness and conveyed us into the kingdom of the Son of His love*" (Colossians 1:13).

When an individual gives possessions or finances as an act of worship or compassion, anointing is released from the heart. The money is transformed by that accompanying anointing into heavenly riches, or *heavenly treasure* laid up in heaven.

> Using money the right way brings
> it under God's control.

## Does God call some individuals to give up wealth and possessions? Yes!

Monks take vows of poverty. Missionaries choose to give up wealth and possessions to serve God on the mission field. A person who goes into the ministry is, in a sense, forfeiting worldly success and finances to serve God. Traditional churches have often provided houses for pastors to partially make up for their meager salary.

A religious attitude in some denominations has sometimes caused congregants to view the poverty of the pastor as a mark of holiness. Although this attitude is extreme, a great many Christian ministers do *voluntarily* sacrifice the pursuit of material wealth to serve God. Some ministers prosper financially, of course, but most have a lower standard of living than individuals in the business world or other professions.

Jesus did not give canned answers, but dealt with individuals differently because He knew what was in their hearts. In Matthew 19:21-22, the rich young ruler who came to Jesus was *ruled* by his wealth. He couldn't let go. Jesus tells him to sell his possessions and give to the poor, but does not tell His friends, Mary and Martha, to give away their house and other possessions.

*Jesus answered, "If you want to be perfect, go, sell your possessions and give to the poor, and you will have treasure in heaven. Then come, follow me." When the young man heard this, he went away sad, because he had great wealth* (Matthew 19:21-22).

---

**God calls some individuals to give up wealth and possessions.**

---

## Does God call other individuals to finance kingdom business? Yes!

Any poor person can stand on the street corner and preach the gospel. However, it takes money to finance the kingdom of God. The key is God calls certain people to do things that take money to accomplish. Kingdom prosperity, however, is for servants of God who are called to fulfill His purposes, not for those who desire wealth for carnal reasons. *"Let the Lord be magnified, Who has pleasure in the prosperity of His servant"* (Psalm 35:27).

Joseph was placed in an exalted position by God and given great wealth, and power over all the land of Egypt. God then used Joseph to provide for his own family and the nation of Israel.

*And Pharaoh said to Joseph, "See, I have set you over all the land of Egypt." Then Pharaoh took his signet ring off his hand and put it on Joseph's hand; and he clothed him in garments of fine linen and put a gold chain around his neck. And he had him ride in the second chariot which he had; and they cried out before him, "Bow the knee!" So he set him over all the land of Egypt* (Genesis 41:41-43).

---

God calls some to finance kingdom business.

---

The Lord funneled a tremendous amount of wealth to and through the hands of John Wesley, who was responsible for transforming the nation of England through his program of discipleship, good works, and charitable institutions such as hospitals, orphanages, and schools.

Because of Wesley, the entire economy of a nation was blessed. Proverbs 13:22 says that God stores up the wealth of the sinner for the righteous: "*The wealth of the sinner is stored up for the righteous.*" At the time of his death, however, Wesley owned little more than the clothes on his back. He gave everything for God. A righteous person is someone who lives for God.

## Property Rights

Have you ever been mugged, robbed, or had your home burglarized? If you yourself haven't been a victim of theft, you probably know someone else who was. How does being robbed make someone feel? It makes them feel *violated*. Why is this? God implanted a sense of right and wrong, theft and personal property, in our heart. God gave us the *natural right* to have our own property. We "buy" property by our own labor so we can purchase the necessities of life for ourselves and our family.

We pay taxes to purchase services such as police protection, having a fire department, and so forth. Everyone agrees to contribute for the common good through paying taxes. When the government, however, picks the pocket of a single mother working two jobs to provide for her children to pay someone else's college tuition, the single mother becomes a victim of *governmental theft*.

## Fill in the Blanks

What would you call someone who broke into your best friend's apartment and stole their wallet? You would call them a _____.

What if they needed the money to pay their bills? They would still be a _____.

If you stole your friend's money, *you* would be a _____.

If the GOVERNMENT takes YOUR money to pay another person's bills, rent, college tuition, student loan, healthcare, or give food stamps, the government is a _____.

*God is your source.* The government is not your source. Again, *God* is your source. If you are a Christian, the Bible says to trust God, not man.

> *It is better to trust in the LORD than to put confidence in man* (Psalm 118:8).

## God commanded the ravens to feed Elijah.

> *So* [Elijah] *went and did according to the word of the LORD, for he went and stayed by the Brook Cherith... The ravens brought him bread and meat in the morning, and bread and meat in the evening; and he drank from the brook* (1 Kings 17:5-6).

## David declared he had NEVER seen the righteous forsaken by God.

> *I have been young, and now am old; Yet I have not seen the righteous forsaken, nor his descendants begging bread* (Psalm 37:25).

---

God gave man the natural right to have property to provide for the necessities of life.

---

*God promises to provide.* Your provision comes from God, and He *promises* to care for you. God says that He will provide for you if you will only trust Him! In Matthew 6:25-26, Jesus says that you don't have to worry.

Your heavenly Father knows what you need and you are of great value to Him.

> *Therefore I say to you, do not worry about your life, what you will eat or what you will drink; nor about your body, what you will put on. Is not life more than food and the body more than clothing? Look at the birds of the air, for they neither sow nor reap nor gather into barns; yet your heavenly Father feeds them. Are you not of more value than they?* (Matthew 6:25-26).

Nowhere in the Bible does God tell anyone to look to the government to give them the necessities of life. God *warns* against trusting man more than Him. That includes government!

> [The Folly of Not Trusting God] *Woe to those who go down to Egypt for help, and rely on horses, who trust in chariots because they are many, and in horsemen because they are very strong, but who do not look to the Holy One of Israel, nor seek the Lord!* (Isaiah 31:1).

God says, when you fail to trust Him as your source, your heart has departed from Him. Anything you depend on more than God is an idol, or a false god. If you look to the government to meet your needs, the government has become your god. Who do you really think *cares* more about you anyway?

God or the government?

*[P]ut your hope in God and know real blessing!
...He always does what He says—He defends
the wronged, He feeds the hungry* (Psalm 146:4
MSG).

---

God warns against trusting man more
than Him. That includes government!

---

When you trust God, your supply will never run out.
Some people, however, sabotage their own provision by
failing to give tithes and offerings to God. God promises
that when you give to Him, He will pour out blessings for
you. If you are faithful in tithes and offerings to demonstrate your trust in God, God assures you that He will
provide for you. Whose *promises* do you believe? God's or
the government's?

*Bring all the tithes into the storehouse, that there
may be food in My house, and* [TEST] *Me now
in this," says the LORD of hosts, "If I will not
open for you the windows of heaven and POUR
OUT for you such blessing that there will not be
room enough to receive it. And I will REBUKE
THE DEVOURER for your sakes"* (Malachi
3:10-11 NASB).

God says He will *"pour out"* a great blessing for those who trust Him and do what is right. In Malachi 3:9, the word "pour out" in Hebrew, *rûwq*, paints a word picture of God opening a window in heaven and pouring out a flow from a pitcher that never stops flowing. Money is caught up into a *spiritual flow*. God says if you give to Him, He will give to you. The river of blessing will never stop flowing as long as you keep giving. It is a supernatural principle with God's guarantee stamped on it!

## CLASH OF KINGDOMS

God is building His kingdom, but satan is building his kingdom, too. Everything that God does is opposed by the enemy. God creates, the devil counterfeits. God creates, the devil destroys. Whenever God initiates something, the enemy designs an evil opposite. God gives life, the devil brings death. God gives prosperity, but satan gives poverty. The kingdom of God is described as a glorious shining city, but the enemy has a corrupt shadow city. These two spiritual realms are at war for dominance, and humans are the foot soldiers.

God gives prosperity, but the devil gives poverty.

## Light and Darkness

*Light.* The Protestant Reformation restored truth to the Church and released the Bible into the hands of the ordinary believers. The old persecutes the new. Christian Protestants were driven out of Europe, and fled for safety to a new land, a safe haven protected by two oceans. They envisioned a nation filled with God's light where men could be free.

*Darkness.* During the Enlightenment, many intellectuals turned away from God to worship human reasoning. American academic elites went to study in Europe, and brought the poisonous seeds of darkness back to America with them. Intelligence can be used for great evil, and the farther removed from God, the more evil it will become.

> This new world hath been the asylum for the persecuted lovers of civil and religious liberty from every part of Europe. Hither have they fled, not from the tender embraces of the mother, but from the cruelty of the monster; and it is so far true of England, that the same tyranny which drove the first emigrants from home, pursues their descendants still.
>
> —THOMAS PAINE, *Common Sense*, 1776

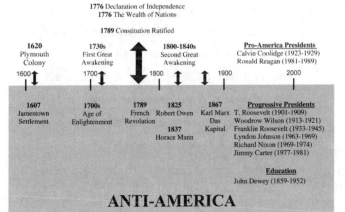

**PRO-AMERICA**
A Shining City on a Hill

1776 Declaration of Independence
1776 The Wealth of Nations

1789 Constitution Ratified

| **1620**<br>Plymouth<br>Colony | **1730s**<br>First Great<br>Awakening | | **1800-1840s**<br>Second Great<br>Awakening | | **Pro-America Presidents**<br>Calvin Coolidge (1923-1929)<br>Ronald Reagan (1981-1989) |

1600   1700   1800   1900   2000

| **1607**<br>Jamestown<br>Settlement | **1700s**<br>Age of<br>Enlightenment | **1789**<br>French<br>Revolution | **1825**<br>Robert Owen<br><br>**1837**<br>Horace Mann | **1867**<br>Karl Marx<br>Das<br>Kapital | **Progressive Presidents**<br>T. Roosevelt (1901-1909)<br>Woodrow Wilson (1913-1921)<br>Franklin Roosevelt (1933-1945)<br>Lyndon Johnson (1963-1969)<br>Richard Nixon (1969-1974)<br>Jimmy Carter (1977-1981) |

**Education**
John Dewey (1859-1952)

**ANTI-AMERICA**

The Conflict between Light and Darkness

## God and Greed

### *Missionaries*

- ***God.*** In the 16th century, God sent missionaries of God's love to North and South America to bring the light of the gospel to the Indians.

- ***Greed.*** The enemy sent Spanish Conquistadors and other explorers, greedy for gold, who killed and subjugated the Indians.

### *Settlers*

- ***God.*** God sent the Plymouth pilgrims to establish a covenantal new land, dedicated to the glory of God. And they were met by Christian Indians who befriended them. They prospered under God's economic principles of free enterprise. God poured out spiritual revivals. He continually turned the heart of America back to Himself by pouring out waves of His Spirit on America for in the First and Second Great Awakenings.

- *Greed.* The enemy sent traders and merchants greedy for wealth to Jamestown. They tried to survive under a form of socialism/communism, many wouldn't work, they stole from the Indians, and most of them died.

## Freedom and Tyranny

- *Freedom.* The American Revolution was a revolution for the cause of freedom under God. In 1776, a new and free nation was born, the United States of America—based on the principles of Christianity and in covenant with God.

Happily for America, happily, we trust, for the whole human race, they pursued a new and more noble course. They accomplished a revolution which has no parallel in the annals of human society.

—JAMES MADISON, *Federalist* No. 14, November 20, 1787

- **Tyranny.** The French had a revolution dedicated to man, not God, and ended up with a Reign of Terror, under the leadership of Maximilien Robespierre. The guillotine became the symbol of the revolutionary cause. Within a year, the French destroyed their own country and brutally murdered an estimated 16,000 to 40,000 people. Will and Ariel Durant gave an account in *The Story of Civilization*:

Most previous revolutions had been against the state or the church, rarely against both at once. ...Is it any wonder that... France went mad. ... The Philosophers had recognized that, having rejected the theological foundations of morality, they were obligated to find another basis, another system of belief that would incline men to decent behavior as citizens, husbands, wives, parents, and children. But they were not at all confident that the human animal could be controlled without a supernaturally sanctioned moral code. Voltaire and [Jean Jacques]

Rousseau finally admitted the moral necessity of popular religious belief.[1]

---

The American revolution was a revolution for the cause of freedom under God!

---

Vladimir Lenin, Joseph Stalin and Adolph Hitler found inspiration for their barbarity in that of Maximilien Robespierre (1758-1794). Robespierre was finally undone by his obsession for creating an ideal government and indifference toward the resulting brutish slaughter of French citizens. Approximately 16,500 men and women were put to death (usually by the guillotine) and around 10,000 died in hellish prisons. Everyone turned against him in the end.

The brutality of the communists and Nazis can be traced back to the deliberate and systematic violence of the French Revolution to crush resistance. However, the pendulum quickly swung from terror and anarchy to tyranny under a revolutionary dictatorship.

## Prosperity and Poverty

### Prosperity

God's principles of economics were published in the first book of modern economic theory in 1776, Adam Smith's *The Wealth of Nations*. America's Founding Fathers were wise enough to design an economic strategy based on Smith's work. America became a model of prosperity.

### Poverty

In 1789 the French Revolution began. The French had already destroyed their own economy by slaughtering the French Huguenots, the Protestants, who made up the nation's middle class—the merchants, businessmen, traders, doctors, and lawyers. They destroyed their entire middle class leaving a non-working aristocracy and an impoverished peasant class. Without a thriving middle class, their economy took a nose dive and led to a bloody revolution. When the starving poor begged for bread, the tone-deaf Queen Marie Antoinette supposedly replied, "Let them eat cake."

---

The American Revolution was a revolution for the cause of freedom under God.

---

## Discussion Questions

1. What makes money good or bad?

2. Does God call some to give away what they have? Why?

3. Does God call others to business and finance? Why?

4. Does the government create wealth? Why or why not?

5. How does government get its money?

6. Compare the clash of good and evil in America in:

   - Light and darkness
   - God and greed
   - Freedom and tyranny
   - Prosperity and poverty

## ENDNOTE

1  Will Durant and Ariel Durant, *The Story of Civilization, Vol. X*, "Rousseau and Revolution" (New York, NY: Simon and Schuster, 1967), 902-903.

# CHAPTER 7

# TEST BY THE WORD OF GOD

*So let each one give as he purposes in*
*his heart, not grudgingly or of necessity;*
*for God loves a cheerful giver.*
—2 CORINTHIANS 9:7

Both supporters and opponents of socialism refer to the Bible to support their position. What does the Bible really say about socialism?

# TEST BY THE WORD: SOCIALISM/COMMUNISM

### What does the Bible say about socialism/communism?

> You shall not COVET your neighbor's wife; and you shall not desire your neighbor's house, his field, his male servant, his female servant, his ox, his donkey, or anything that is your neighbor's (Deuteronomy 5:21).

A thief takes something belonging to someone else, without their permission. The Ten Commandments say that it is wrong to take someone else's property. When the government takes money from citizens by coercion, it is stealing from them. "*You shall not STEAL*" (Deuteronomy 5:19).

God gets even more specific by saying it is a sin to even *think* about wanting what someone else owns. If you *want* something that belongs to someone else, you are sinning. So, when individuals demand that the rich be taxed more to give handouts to *them*, they are coveting the property of others. Socialism breeds sin.

### God, not government, is the source of all provision

> The LORD has blessed my blessed my master [Abraham] *greatly and he has become great;*

*and He has given him flocks and herds, silver and gold, male and female servants, and camels and donkeys* (Genesis 24:35).

### Be content with what God gives you

*Let your conduct be without covetousness; be content with such things as you have. For He Himself has said, "I will never leave you nor forsake you"* (Hebrews 13:5).

### Everyone should work for what he or she gets

*If anyone will not WORK, neither shall he eat* (2 Thessalonians 3:10).

---

You shall not STEAL. You shall not COVET.

---

## TEST BY THE WORD: FREE ENTERPRISE

The Bible addresses financial matters more often than prayer, healing, and mercy. God is not against money. He is just against the improper use of it. Seventeen of the 36 parables of Jesus are concerned with property and stewardship. Although we may think of wealth in terms of an abundance of material possessions, in the Bible wealth is much more than worldly things. It is the sum total of all that God has provided for us to have a satisfying blessed life while we are here on earth. *"O LORD, how manifold are Your works! In wisdom You have made them all. The earth is full of Your possessions"* (Psalm 104:24).

---

God is not against money. He is just against the improper use of it.

---

## God Owns the Whole World

We don't really own anything, but have access to what is lent to us by God. We are stewards of what belongs to Him. In Psalm 50:12, God says, *"For the world is Mine, and all its fullness."*

*God gives property to people.* Scripture teaches the importance of private property. Psalm 115:16 says, *"The heaven, even the heavens, are the LORD's; But the earth He has given to the children of men."* Although the earth belongs to God, God gives man the right to have a portion of His property to provide the necessities of life. If something is *given* to you, it is your *private property*. You own it. If anyone takes your property from you, they have committed a crime. God says it is sin to steal someone's property. Property and property rights are important to God.

A three-year-old child objects if another child takes their toy. Children understand the concept of "mine." Although you may teach children to share, you assure them that their toy will be returned. You also teach them that when they give a birthday gift to a friend, the gift becomes the friend's *property.*

- God gives property and land for man to use.

  *Then the LORD appeared to Abram and said, "To your descendants I will give this land"* (Genesis 12:7).

- The Eighth Commandment, *"You shall not steal,"* reveals that God considers private property to be important. God forbids stealing what belongs to another person.

- The Tenth Commandment, *"You shall not covet,"* commands us to not even THINK about stealing property belonging to another person.

*Man is a steward of God's wealth.* Wealth is a gift from God. It was created by God and it belongs to God. Everything in the earth, in the ground, above the ground, in the air belongs to God. The gold in every gold mine is owned by God. "*The silver is Mine, and the gold is Mine,' says the LORD of Hosts"* (Haggai 2:8).

*The earth is the LORD's, and all its fullness, the world and those who dwell therein* (Psalm 24:1).

We are stewards of *God's* wealth. He is watching what we do with it. He allows us to use what we need to live on, but we are to invest the rest so that it will bring an increase.

*God ordained work.* The principle of work is found in the book of Genesis. In Genesis 1:1-15, God Himself is working. He created the heavens, the stars and planets, the seas, and everything on earth. God worked for six days and rested on the seventh day. God was the first to do any work on the earth. Therefore, legitimate work for man reflects the activity of God. Because God is good, work is also good.

---

God ordained work for man to gain wealth.

---

Also, in Genesis 1:31, Amplified Bible translation, God assessed the *quality* of His work. He was satisfied with what He had accomplished, and was pleased with the result: *"And God saw everything that He had made, and behold, it was very good...and He approved it completely."*

> *The Lord God took the man and put him in the garden of Eden to work it and keep it* (Genesis 2:15).

> *When you eat the labor of your hands, you shall be happy, and it shall be well with you* (Psalm 128:2).

*A good man makes a profit.* God does not want us to *love* money, but He does want us to be blessed and prosperous. Proverbs 13:22 says a good man should profit so much from his labor that he leaves an inheritance.

> *A GOOD man leaves an inheritance to his children's children, but the sinner's wealth is laid up for the righteous* (Proverbs 13:22).

Whether or not you realize it, many individuals in the Bible were rich. We are told that Abram was *"extremely rich"* in Genesis 13:2. Jacob was *"very wealthy"* (see Genesis 30:43), and Isaac became a very rich man and *"his wealth continued to grow"* (Genesis 26:13).

In Genesis 13:2, we learn that King David had incredible wealth, and in 1 Chronicles 29:3, we discover that he was able to give all the gold and silver for the building of the Temple, an enormous amount in today's terms. The Queen of Sheba visited King Solomon and was left breathless when she saw the extent of his wealth. God demonstrated that He had no difficulty getting wealth into the hands of faithful stewards to accomplish His purposes.

---

According to the Bible, a good man makes a profit.

---

*God has a plan to fill the earth with His glory.* When man sinned, he lost the covering of God's glory. Since that time, God has wanted His glory to be released on earth again.

> *Truly, as I live, all the earth shall be filled with the glory of the LORD* (Numbers 14:21).

*It takes money to fill the earth with God's glory.* Any poor man can preach the gospel but it takes wealth to transform a nation. Although God wants to bless us personally, money has a mission, and God is looking for willing partners to complete this mission. John Wesley wrote in one of his sermons:

> When the possessor of Heaven and Earth brought you into being and placed you in this world, He placed you here not as an owner but as a steward. As such, He entrusted you for a season with goods of various kinds. But the sole property of these still rests in Him nor can ever be alienated from Him, as you are not your own but His. Such as likewise all you enjoy.[1]

As mentioned previously, John Wesley was such a faithful steward the entire nation of England was transformed through his faithful use of finances and Christian discipleship. Vast sums of money were given to him but that wealth was channeled into schools, orphanages, hospitals, and many other charitable institutions and good deed. Wesley himself died with few worldly goods of his own. Everything that God gave to Wesley was used to establish the work of God.

*The Spirit of God is the Spirit of the Creator.* God gives man *power* to get wealth. In Deuteronomy 8:18, the word "power" in the original Hebrew is *koach*, which means *to create together, to produce, to industrialize* to get wealth. God is the Creator. His Spirit is a *creating* spirit. Man has been given the privilege to co-labor with God in creation by receiving revelation for wealth creation.

---

Any poor man can preach the gospel but
it takes wealth to transform a nation.

---

*God prospers His servants to establish His covenant.* What is God's ultimate purpose for wealth? To advance the kingdom of God on earth. And that takes money! He blesses mankind with the ability to get wealth so that, by using this money, God can bring the nations of the earth into covenant with Him.

> *And you shall remember the LORD your God, for it is He who gives you POWER* [Hb. Koach: to create together, to produce, to industrialize] *to get wealth, that He may establish His covenant* (Deuteronomy 8:18).

*There are many forms of stealing.* Scripture mandates that all measurements and standards should be accurate, consistent, and unchanging, customers won't be cheated (see Leviticus 19:35-36). The Bible forbids cheating or defrauding others (see Leviticus 19:13). The Scriptures also prohibit moving markers that define land boundaries (see Deuteronomy 19:14-20).

- Free enterprise: Property is protected
- Socialism/communism: Property is plundered

## Property is the Foundation for the Rule of Law

Why must government protect rights? Because God gave man rights. These are *rights given to man by God Himself.* The *Bill of Rights* is a written guarantee that the rights of American citizens would not be violated. It was designed to limit *governmental reach* into the lives of private citizens. It was never intended to be used against individuals.

*Protection of rights is one of the purposes for government.* God gives man the right to life and the right to own property. Man pays his own time and effort to earn property, so it is his right to keep what he has purchased with part of his life. It is wrong for another individual or government to take what you own.

*A person "pays" his time and labor (the currency of life) to purchase property.* What was happening in the American colonies concerning property prior to the Revolutionary War? The British were engaging in arbitrary seizure of people's property and levying excessive taxes, fines, duties and tariffs. Imagine what it would be like if you no longer had any right to own, keep, or protect what you have. Your neighbor, a looter, or the government could take whatever they wished.

---

"We cannot be free without being secure in our property."

---

In his 1828 dictionary, Noah Webster defined property as "the exclusive right of possessing, enjoying and disposing of a thing; ownership." And, "In the beginning the Creator gave man dominion over the earth, over the fish of the sea and the fowls of the air, and over every living thing. This is the foundation of man's property in the earth and in all its productions."[2]

John Dickinson, signer of the Constitution, wrote, "Let these truths be indelibly impressed on our minds: (1) that we cannot be happy without being free; (2) that we cannot be free without being secure in our property; (3) that we cannot be secure in our property if without our consent others may as by right take it away."[3]

- If an individual steals property it is a crime.
- If a government steals property it is a crime.

  *You who preach that a man should not steal, do you steal?"* (Romans 2:21b).

- If it is morally wrong for an individual, it is morally wrong for a government.
- Socialism/communism is LEGALIZED THEFT.
- Socialism makes SIN lawful.
- The law itself becomes an IMMORAL instrument of theft.

## Socialism Is Anti-Christ

- Socialism attacks the religious beliefs of Christians and Jews.
- Socialism teaches that all Bible-believers are enemies of socialism. (They are right!)
- Socialism crushes creativity.

## Socialism Is Morally Wrong

Socialism:

- Teaches it is wrong to prosper and profit.
- Steals from some to give to others.
- Extinguishes personal motivation and incentive.
- Destroys the individual work ethic.
- Makes sin legal.

God emphasizes the *moral excellence* of free enterprise. He praises the *virtuous* woman for hard work, diligence, doing business, and making a profit.

*She also rises while it is yet night, and provides
food for her household, and a portion for her
maidservants. She considers a field and buys it;
from her profits she plants a vineyard* (Proverbs
31:15-16).

## The Prosperity of Israel

The Israel of Jesus' day was still a land of "milk and honey"
with fertile farmlands,[4] grassy hills "clothed with flocks,"
and rivers teeming with fish. Literature and archaeo-
logical finds substantiate that it was wealthy in forests,
abundant in all types of natural resources, and an exporter
of fruit, wine, olives, grain, spices and oils.[5] It was one of
the prized possessions held by the Roman empire!

> The Israel of Jesus' day was still
> a land of "milk and honey."

The towns and cities in the time of Jesus were known
for the finest examples of engineering and architecture.
Sepphoris, three miles from Nazareth, "had all the trap-
pings of a modern, wealthy city of the Roman Empire. It
boasted an elaborate water system with a cistern a thousand feet long."[6] Homes of the day were not all minimal
dirt floor dwellings, as often depicted in Sunday school
pictures, although there *were* simple peasant houses,
especially in rural areas.

For the most affluent Israelites, city dwellings were often multiple story dwellings with courtyards and beautiful architectural stonework and details. Houses were constructed with columns, atriums, interior courtyards, and mosaics, often with Roman influence, and commonly plastered inside and out with lime plaster.[7]

Israel was also the "crossroads of the ancient world." The main trade route of the civilized world, the Via Maris, passed through it. One of the finest examples of the skill used in city building was found in Caesarea Maritima. It was one of the most renowned seaports of its day, with a forty-acre natural harbor, complete with a lighthouse to guide ships. "Much of the city was built with imported marble and the city had an elaborate sewer system that was cleansed by the sea."[8]

Israel was the "crossroads of the ancient world."

During the centuries following the destruction of Jerusalem, Israel was de-forested and ruined. This resulted in soil erosion in large areas. It was also a common custom for conquering armies to sow the land with salt to destroy the soil. "The Turks dealt the final blow in the period of the first world war, when they cut down the last remnants of the forests to keep the railways running!"[9]

> *I will bring the land to desolation, and your*
> *enemies who dwell in it shall be astonished at it.*
> *I will scatter you among the nations and draw*
> *out a sword after you; your land shall be deso-*
> *late and your cities waste* (Leviticus 26:32-33).

The land of Israel remained in this sad state until the return of the Jews to the land following World War I. They began the hard work of reclaiming the land. It was no small task, but once more it can be said:

> *The wilderness and the wasteland shall be glad*
> *for them, and the desert shall rejoice and blos-*
> *som as the rose* (Isaiah 35:1).

## Jesus and Business

When Joseph and Mary journeyed to Bethlehem to pay taxes before the birth of Jesus, they weren't homeless or destitute. If they had to pay taxes, they had money. Although they had planned to stay in an inn, there was no vacancy because Bethlehem was flooded with travelers at that time.

Joseph, the earthly father of Jesus, may not have been just a maker of simple, wooden furniture, as he has often been portrayed. In the Gospels, the word *tekton* is used to describe Joseph (Matthew 13:55; cf., Mark 6:3). A *tekton*, "a carpenter who builds," was not just an ordinary carpenter, but more like a general contractor, described by

Paul in First Corinthians 3:10 as a *"wise master builder."*[10] Rocks and cut stone were the main building materials of the day, rather than wood, so a *tekton* would work as a stonemason, often using local limestone and imported marble.[11] However, even if Joseph did just make furniture, he was still a small business owner.

Hebrew families often lived in family housing complexes called *insulae* (singular *insula*) designed for a multi-generational extended family, constructed around an open courtyard. The insula is referenced in the New Testament as "household," meaning "an extended family living together."[12] It is possible Jesus, and perhaps His brothers, worked alongside Joseph to construct their own family home.

> *Where did this Man* [Jesus] *get this wisdom and these mighty works? Is this not the carpenter's* [Gk. tekton] *son? Is not His mother called Mary? And His brothers James, Joses, Simon, and Judas? And His sisters, are they not all with us? Where then did this Man get all these things?" So they were offended at Him* (Matthew 13:54-57).

Joseph was a small business owner.

Contrary to popular mythology, therefore, it is unlikely Jesus was a poor man. Even if His family wasn't wealthy, they were almost certainly comfortably middle class. It is not stated in the Bible, but Joseph and his sons would surely have hired other workers, craftsmen, and artisans during construction, as was the common practice at that time. The eldest son was expected to take over the family business someday, so Jesus would have learned skills for building as well as good business practices from Joseph.

When Jesus taught the parable of "the Wise and Foolish Builders, speaking of a house built on a rock instead of sand," He understood the importance of building on a proper foundation from experience. Jesus also called Himself the *Cornerstone* and said He is the *builder* of His church, using *living stones* as the building material.

> *Therefore everyone who hears these words of mine and puts them into practice is like **a wise man who built his house on the rock**. The rain came down, the streams rose, and the winds blew and beat against that house; yet it did not fall, because it had its foundation on the rock* (Matthew 7:24 NIV).

> *Jesus Christ Himself being **the chief cornerstone, in whom the whole building, being fitted together**, grows into a holy temple in the Lord, in whom you also are being built together for a dwelling place of God in the Spirit* (Ephesians 4:19-22).

> *[O]n this rock I will build* My *church* (Matthew 16:17).
>
> *Coming to Him as to a **living stone**, rejected indeed by men, but chosen by God and precious, you also, as living stones, are being built up a spiritual house* (1 Peter 4:2).

---

## Jesus was a capitalist!

---

In the Parable of the Minas, Luke 19:11-26, Jesus praises those who buy, sell, and trade. He tells the parable of a master who gives each one a certain amount of money and commands them to "do business." Jesus encourages his disciples to become successful entrepreneurs.

Jesus was a *capitalist!*

### The master provides servants with money

The master provides them with some of his own property, giving each a *mina*. How much was a mina worth? One mina was roughly the value of twenty years work by an ordinary person. He entrusted them with a lot of money!

### God's servants are expected to do business

The ten servants are clearly expected to do business with this money. Therefore, the master has confidence that they have both ability and opportunity. Luke 19:11-26 says:

*Now as they heard these things, [Jesus] spoke another parable, because He was near Jerusalem and because they thought the kingdom of God would appear immediately. Therefore He said: "A certain nobleman went into a far country to receive for himself a kingdom and to return. So he called **ten of his servants**, delivered to them **ten minas**, and said to them, '**Do business** till I come.'"*

## The master asks for an accounting

When the master returns after a long absence, he asks his servants to tell him how they had done.

*And so it was that when he returned, having received the kingdom, he then commanded these servants, to whom he had given the money, to be called to him, that he might know how much every man had gained by trading* (Luke 19:15).

## The first servant is praised and rewarded

The first servant is praised by the master. Of all the servants, this is the only one to whom the master says "well done" and calls him "faithful." Then the master gives the servant a significant reward for his faithfulness, "have authority over ten cities."

*Then came the first, saying, "Master, your mina has earned ten minas." And he said to him, "Well done, good servant; because you were faithful in a very little, have authority over ten cities"* (Luke 19:16).

---

The master asks his servants
to give an accounting.

---

### The next servant is only rewarded

The next servant receives a reward of authority over five cities, but the master does not tell him "well done." He receives a reward but is not praised.

> *And the second came, saying, "Master, your mina has earned five minas." Likewise he said to him, "You also be over five cities"* (Luke 19:18-19).

### The last servant is reprimanded

The final servant comes to the master with an excuse. The servant accurately states that the master is an austere man, because the master agrees with this assessment. The word *austere* means "demanding hard work and diligent carefulness." The last servant confesses that he didn't even try to do business, but put his mina in storage.

> *Then another came, saying, "Master, here is your mina, which I have kept put away in a handkerchief. For I feared you, because you are an austere man* [demanding hard work and diligent carefulness]. *You collect what you did*

*not deposit, and reap what you did not sow"*
(Luke 19:20-21).

This servant is reprimanded for being lazy and non-productive. The master calls him *wicked*. He neither engaged in hard work nor was he diligent. Was there no one who could advise him, no one who could mentor him in business and investing? He certainly could have asked the other servants to give him some financial advice!

> *And he said to him, "Out of your own mouth I will judge you, you wicked servant. You knew that I was an austere man, collecting what I did not deposit and reaping what I did not sow. Why then did you not put my money in the bank, that at my coming I might have collected it with interest?"* (Luke 19:22-23).

## The master is not a *socialist*

What does the master do? He doesn't make the other servants give some of their money to the unprofitable servant. Instead, takes the servant's money from him and gives it to those who did make a profit!

## "From those who do nothing, even what little they have will be taken away."

The master does not take from the *haves* to give to the *have-not*. Instead, the master takes from the have-not and gives it to the one who prospered.

*Then, turning to the others standing nearby, the king ordered, "Take the money from this servant, and give it to the one who has ten pounds." "But, master," they said, "he already has ten pounds!" "Yes," the [master] replied, "and **to those who use well what they are given, even more will be given. But from those who do nothing, even what little they have will be taken away"** (Luke 19:24-26 NLT).*

---

The master takes from the have-not and gives it to the one who prospered the most.

---

## TEST BY THE WORD: CHARITY AND THE POOR

Jesus Himself tells us that the poor will always be with us. Life is not fair. We have no guarantee of equal outcome, equal talent, or equal wealth.

*For you have the poor with you always, and whenever you wish you may do them good* (Mark 14:7).

---

"You have the poor with you always"

---

Therefore, what, then, does the Bible say to do about the *poor?* Help them, of course. But God also tells us *how*. He has provided us with an opportunity to sow good deeds, care for our fellowman, and lay up *for ourselves treasure in heaven through acts of charity.*

> *Do not neglect to do good and to share what you have, for such sacrifices are pleasing to God* (Hebrews 13:16)

> *Blessed are those who are generous, because they feed the poor* (Proverbs 22:9).

What is *charity*? Charity is *voluntary* provision of help or relief based on goodwill and love of one's fellowman. Charity is a matter of the heart. Only individuals can do charity, because charity requires genuine love or it is worthless to God.

> *And though I bestow all my goods to feed the poor....but have not love, it profits me nothing* (Corinthians 13:3).

If this is the case, the government *cannot* do charity. It is actually unconstitutional for the government to redistribute the wealth of U.S. citizens to benefit one group of people more than another group.

> *Each one must give as he has decided in his heart, not reluctantly or under compulsion, for God loves a cheerful giver* (2 Corinthians 9:7).

## Does the Bible Teach Socialism?

Acts 4:32-35 is sometimes quoted to claim that Jesus taught socialism. What do these verses actually teach?

First, in the Book of Acts Christians were supernaturally knit together into a *one accord* that was so powerful that they were *"of one heart and soul."* Secondly, they had received an impartation of "great grace." The word for great in Greek is *megas*. They had received an extraordinary measure of grace, or *mega-grace*. To have all things in common, these believers needed supernatural help.

> *Now the full number of those who believed were* ***of one heart and soul****, and no one said that any of the things that belonged to him was his own, but they had everything in common. And with great power the apostles were giving their testimony to resurrection of the Lord Jesus, and* ***GREAT GRACE*** *was upon them all* (Acts 4:32-33).

Finally, they laid all they had at the feet of the *apostles*—NOT the civil government! God has given the responsibility for charitable giving to the *church*! There is a big difference between the first-century apostolic church and civil government. Moreover, they were not REQUIRED, taxed, or forced to give. They gave voluntarily.

> *There was not a needy person among them, for as many as were owners of lands or houses sold them and brought the proceeds of what was sold and laid it at the* ***apostles' feet*** [NOT THE

CIVIL GOVERNMENT] *and it was distrib- uted to each as any had need* (Acts 4:34-35).

---

They laid all they had at the feet of the apostles—NOT the civil government!

---

## A Unique Situation

To fully understand this period of time in the early church, we must look back to Passover and the Day of Pentecost when the church was born. At the time Jesus ascended, He had been with His disciples for 40 days following the resurrection. Before departing, Jesus directed His disciples to wait in Jerusalem until they were endued with power. Another ten days takes us to Pentecost— Sunday morning, AD 30.

Sunday morning started gloriously. The Holy Spirit fell upon the 120 praying in the upper room, Peter preached his first sermon, and 3,000 were instantly added to the church. Now the church numbered 3,120. How awesome!

When Monday morning dawned, church life began in earnest. But there were big problems that needed to be solved. Things were messy. Scores of out-of-towners had poured into Jerusalem for Passover and were still in Jerusalem for the Feast of Pentecost. Some had left, but most stayed. The city was packed with visitors. If it had been any other year, the celebrants would have begun returning to their homes in Judea, Galilee, and other countries on this day.

Travelers had only packed for a short stay with some clothes and a little money for the trip. Now what were they to do? They didn't want to leave, but how could they stay in Jerusalem without food, houses, or jobs? Most new church members were broke and homeless! This was just the first day, and many more would soon be added to their number.

---

Travelers were broke and homeless!

---

Where could that many people meet together? And where and how would they live? The solution to the first problem was relatively simple. The church could assemble at Solomon's porch outside the Temple. The second predicament was a bit more complex. It is probable that having all things in common began here. They *had* to depend on one another simply to survive. Those who had homes in Jerusalem opened them to visitors and shared their food. Those who had material and financial resources helped those in need.

*It was years before any other churches were planted.* For perhaps eight to twelve years the church stayed right there in Jerusalem. Then Gentiles began to be added to their number, churches sprang up in Judea, and missionary journeys began. When the circumstances changed and churches were planted in other locations, believers were expected to get jobs and provide for themselves.

This particular pattern of *"all things in common"* began and ended here in the Jerusalem. It was the *exception* rather than the rule. Soon, Paul would say, "Those unwilling to work will not get to eat (2 Thessalonians 3:10 NLT).

## The Founding Fathers on Socialism

> The moment the idea is admitted into society that property is not as sacred as the laws of God, and that there is not a force of law and public justice to protect it, anarchy and tyranny commence. IF "Thou shalt not covet" and "Thou shalt not steal" were not commandments of Heaven, they must be made inviolable precepts in every society before it can be civilized or made free.
>
> —JOHN ADAMS, *A Defense of the Constitutions of Government of the United States of America*, 1787

> I am for doing good to the poor, but I differ in opinion of the means. I think the best way of doing good to the poor, is not making them

easy in poverty, but leading or driving them out of it.

—BENJAMIN FRANKLIN, *The London Chronicle*, November 29, 1766

A wise and frugal government...shall restrain men from injuring one another, shall leave them otherwise free to regulate their own pursuits of industry and improvement, and shall not take from the mouth of labor the bread it has earned. This is the sum of good government.

—THOMAS JEFFERSON, first inaugural address, March 4, 1801

If we can prevent the government from wasting the labors of the people, under the pretence of taking care of them, they must become happy.

—THOMAS JEFFERSON, letter to Thomas Cooper, November 29, 1802

Persons and property are the two great subjects on which Governments are to act; and that the rights of persons, and the rights of property, are the objects, for the protection of which Government was instituted. These rights cannot well be separated.

—JAMES MADISON, speech at the Virginia Convention, December 2, 1829

## Discussion Questions

1. What does the Bible say about socialism/communism?

2. Who created and owns wealth?

3. What does that make man in regard to wealth?

4. What means did God ordain for man to get wealth? Why?

5. What does it take to fill the earth with God's glory? Why?

6. What divine attribute did God give to man so he could get wealth?

7. What is the foundation for the rule of law? Why?

8. Socialism causes what two sins?

9. Explain why socialism is anti-Christ.

10. Joseph, the husband of Mary, was a *tekton*. What does that mean?

11. In what way was Jesus an *entrepreneur*?

12. Who does the master praise in the parable of the minas?

13. Who does the master take from to reward another?

14. What did the faithful servant do that brought such a reward?

15. Was Jesus a socialist?

## Endnotes

1. John Wesley, *John Wesley's Sermons: An Anthology*. "The Use of Money" (Nashville, TN: Abingdon Press, 1991), 347-358.

2. Noah Webster, *An American Dictionary of the English Language* (New York, NY: S. Converse, 1828).

3. John Dickinson (1801), *The Political Writings of John Dickinson, Vol. I* (Wilmington, DE: Bonsal and Niles, 1801), 275.

4. Ray Vander Laan (2009), *Life and Ministry of the Messiah Discovery Guide (*Grand Rapids, MI: Zondervan, 2009), 122.

5. Ibid., 34-35.

6. Ibid., 34.

7. Ralph Gower, *The New Manners and Customs of Bible Times* (Chicago, IL: The Moody Bible Institute of Chicago, 1987), 38-39.

8. Vander Laan, 34.

9. Lance Lambert, *Israel: The Unique Land, The Unique People* (Carol Stream, IL: Tyndale House Living Books, 1981), 48.

10. Vander Laan, 189-190.

11. Ibid., 122.
12. Ibid., 122-123.

# CHAPTER 8

# TEST BY THE FRUIT

*However beautiful the strategy, you
should occasionally look at the results.*
—Winston Churchill

J esus tells us that we should be fruit inspectors. A good
tree bears good fruit. A bad tree bears bad fruit.

> *You will know them by their fruits. ...A good
> tree cannot bear bad fruit, nor can a bad tree
> bear good fruit* (Matthew 7:16, 19).

*The fruit of free enterprise.* The source of free enterprise
is the Word of God and the Spirit of God. The fruit of
free enterprise is always **prosperity**.

*The fruit of socialism.* The source of socialism is human reasoning and spirit of humanism (evil). The fruit of socialism (and communism) is **poverty and misery**.

A good tree bears good fruit.
A bad tree bears bad fruit.

## THE STANDARD OF LIVING FRUIT

Capitalism directly increases per capita income, raising the standard of living wherever it is practiced. A free society significantly decreases poverty and increases prosperity for the entire population. When there is limited government interference, free enterprise allows people to determine their own standard of living based on aptitude, perseverance, and work ethic.

In a capitalistic economy, people believe they can improve their standard of living by hard work. When the standard of living improves for individuals, the economy of the nation improves. Free enterprise creates a large middle class with mobility between levels of society. Poor individuals are able to lift themselves out of poverty and members of the middle class can become wealthy.

## Economic Freedom and Standard of Living

$63,588

$47,742

GDP per capita for each category of the 2019 Index of Economic Freedom, in constant U.S. dollars

$22,382

$7,829

$7,716

| Free | Mostly Free | Moderately Free | Mostly Unfree | Repressed |

Source: Terry Miller, Anthony Kim, and James Roberts, *2019 Index of Economic Freedom*[1]

## THE CREATIVITY FRUIT

The necessary ingredients for creativity to flourish are an atmosphere that (1) rewards success and hard work, (2) allows competition for excellence, and (3) celebrates individualism. When people have a reason to dream with a reasonable possibility of achievement, human creativity is unleashed. If people feel there is no chance to succeed, they stop trying.

| CAPITALISM | SOCIALISM |
| --- | --- |
| Rewards success | Punishes success |
| Rewards hard work | Rewards laziness |
| Promotes excellence | Promotes mediocrity |
| Encourages individual creativity | Encourages group conformity |
| Protects private property | Plunders private property |
| Guards individual rights | Violates individual rights |
| Limits government control | Expands government control |

*Individual creativity.* Free enterprise rewards creativity by rewarding success and hard work, promoting excellence, encouraging individual creativity, protecting both property rights and individual rights, and having limited governmental regulation.

*Group conformity.* Socialism crushes creativity by punishing success, rewarding laziness, promoting mediocrity and group conformity, violating property and individual rights, and having burdensome government regulations.

Have you heard the often-repeated myth that we are using up the planet's valuable natural resources and the world is facing a crisis? This has been said so often most people probably believe it. Without human creativity there are no resources. *The Ultimate Resource 2,* by Julian Simon, reveals the truth. If you read this book, you will completely reset your thinking.[2]

Of course, God has given us the responsibility to be good stewards of His property, planet earth. That is not the point. Certainly, it is wrong to set forest fires and pollute lakes and rivers. It is wrong to be wasteful and destructive. However, the alarmists are not being truthful. For example, one particular film[3] shown in elementary school classrooms tells children, "In the United States, we have less than four percent of our original forests left." However, according to the U.S. Forest service, 33 percent of America is forested and has been stable for one hundred years! The film also states, "The USA is five percent of global population, but uses 30 percent of resources." This is true, but very misleading. The United States also produces almost 30 percent of the world's GDP. This demonstrates we are *remarkably efficient*, not wasteful!

---

### Without human creativity, there are no resources.

---

The truth of the matter is that every material classified today as a natural resource was once considered useless or even a downright nuisance. Only human creativity could make apparently worthless materials marketable and beneficial. Without human creativity, there are no resources. The *human spirit* is the ultimate resource!

Crude oil became a resource only when someone first creatively figured out that it can be used to satisfy human wants. And even then our ability to use it became a reality only because many other people creatively devised each of the various tools and processes necessary for extracting and refining crude oil. ... Anything that hampers human creativity is thus a curse to all humankind. Anything that encourages human creativity is a boon.[4]

Freedom to create coupled with free enterprise to finance dreams are the necessary ingredients to take what most people would consider impractical or impossible and turn one generation's daydreams into the next generation's necessities.

---

The human spirit is the ultimate resource!

---

## The Prosperity Fruit

History has demonstrated that the fruit of free enterprise is **prosperity**. The fruit of socialism/communism is always **poverty and misery**. For example, the American Indian tribes who receive the most government "help" live as wards of the state on reservations with a poverty rate of 25 percent. However, the Lumbee tribe of Robeson County, North Carolina, is not eligible for the help other tribes receive because the government does not recognize them as sovereign.

The Lumbees open their own businesses, own their own homes, and most do not desire handouts. They are self-sufficient, industrious, and very prosperous capitalists. A Lumbee businessman, Ben Chavis, commented that the Indians on the reservation do so poorly because they "have been trained to be communists."[5]

*Socialism divides the pie.* Socialism says that there is a fixed amount of wealth that must be redistributed. When you believe there is only one pie, how can it be divided up equally so everyone can have a "fair share"? This concept stirs up envy toward those who have a bigger "piece of the pie." Redistribution of wealth requires coercive taking from those with "bigger pieces" to give to others who have less. Unfortunately, the more times the pie is divided, the smaller the pieces become.

*Free enterprise makes more pies.* Free enterprise, on the other hand, offers a much better solution. Rather than re-dividing the pie into smaller and smaller pieces, free enterprise *makes more pies!* Free enterprise is the *only* system that actually creates *more* wealth instead of just shifting around what people already have.

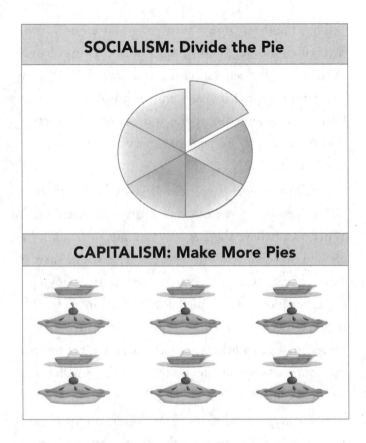

## SOCIALISM/COMMUNISM POVERTY FRUIT

*Jamestown*

In June of 1606, King James I granted a charter to a group of entrepreneurs, the London Company, to plant a settlement at Jamestown, Virginia. In 1607, they sent a group of businessmen to set up a colony in Virginia. The settlers were told to follow these rules of communal living:

- No private property
- Communal living
- Leader assigns tasks

They took no women and only one clergyman. Many of the men who went were British gentlemen who refused to work because they considered work to be beneath their station in life. The first group totally perished. More settlers were sent but, needless to say, they also fared very poorly. They survived by stealing from the Indians. Although they attempted a cover-up, eventually the truth leaked out and reports made it back to Europe. *Communism was unsuccessful in the Jamestown settlement!*

## Plymouth

A company of Pilgrims set out for a new land for freedom of religion. Upon reaching the shores of Cape Cod in 1620, the first action taken by the Pilgrims was to draft the Mayflower Compact, forming a civil government based on covenant with God and with one another. The London Company tried the communism strategy again by giving the same rules to the Pilgrims. Surely Christians in the Plymouth Colony would be able to succeed at communal living more easily than the Jamestown settlers. The settlers were told to follow these same rules of communal living:

- No private property

- Communal living
- Leader assigns tasks

But Christian communism didn't work even with this level of commitment to God and one another. I dare say, most of us believers would look shallow and carnal compared to such courage and devotion. If the Pilgrims couldn't make communism work, who could?

Unfortunately, nearly half of the settlement starved the first winter. People complained about their assigned tasks, some claimed exemption due to disabilities, and Governor William Bradford noticed that those who worked the least showed up with the biggest baskets to collect their share of the food. Christian communism was unsuccessful in the Plymouth colony!

Those who worked the least showed up with the biggest baskets to collect food.

Bradford then went to the Bible and came up with a new plan based on God's principles for prosperity. This changed the entire economic system of the colony. Each family was given their own land to work.

- Families must provide for themselves.
- Anything they produced was their own property.

- If they didn't work, then they had nothing to eat.

The transformation was astounding. Everyone went into the fields willingly and worked diligently. They later held a thanksgiving feast to celebrate the great bounty and to bless God for His provision.

The Plymouth colony thrived under the free enterprise system as the basis for a successful economic policy. These same principles eventually made America the wealthiest and most innovative nation on earth. The Pilgrims sowed the seeds of political freedom, free enterprise, and healthy individualism in covenant with God.

## THE CHARITY FRUIT

Are Americans more or less charitable than citizens of other countries? No developed country even begins to approach American giving. Americans donate three-and-a-half times more to charity than the French. They give seven times more than the Germans, and fourteen times more than the Italians. Americans are 15 percent more likely to volunteer time to help others than the Dutch, 21 percent more likely than the Swiss, and 32 percent more likely than the Germans.

### Who Really Cares?

In his book, *Who Really Cares: The Surprising Truth About Compassionate Conservatism*, Arthur C. Brooks presents research showing that religious conservatives (those who attend church regularly) are much more charitable, compassionate, and willing to volunteer than secular liberals.[6]

Who really cares? Individuals who lean toward socialism give almost none of their *own* money to charity. They just like to give away other people's money. Those who believe *government* should redistribute income are among the *least likely* to donate, volunteer, or help others in any way. Individuals who are religious American *capitalists* turn out to be the biggest givers of all. In an analysis of fifteen sets of data, the conclusion was always the same.

---

Individuals who lean toward socialism give almost none of their own money to charity.

---

Religious American capitalists are much more likely to be generous to those in need than those who believe in socialism. They are twenty-three times more likely to volunteer their time to assist others than socialists. Religious Americans who believe in free enterprise give 75 percent more to charity than Americans who lean toward socialism.

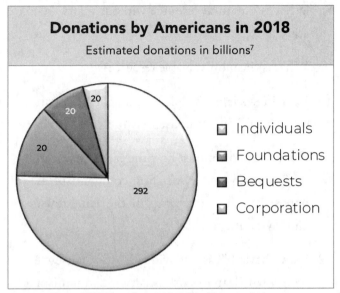

**Donations by Americans in 2018**
Estimated donations in billions[7]

20

20

20

292

□ Individuals
■ Foundations
■ Bequests
□ Corporation

Source: Giving USA Foundation 2019. Used by permission

## Discussion Questions

1. What happens when the standard of living improves for individuals?

2. What is the benefit of a large middle class?

3. Finish the sentence: The necessary ingredients for creativity are an atmosphere that....

4. How does socialism punish creativity?

5. How does free enterprise reward creativity?

7. Is it true that we are using up the planet's natural resources?

8. What is a natural resource without man's creativity?

9. What is the most valuable resource?

10. Explain socialism's "pie" argument? Explain capitalism's "pie" response.

11. Compare and contrast how the early American settlers fared under socialism/communism as opposed to free enterprise in the Jamestown and Plymouth colonies.

12. How charitable are individuals with their own money who lean toward socialism/communism with their own money?

13. Who are the most generous Americans? Why do you think this is true?

## Endnotes

1. Terry Miller, Anthony B. Kim, and James M. Roberts, "2019 Index of Economic Freedom," (Washington DC: *The Heritage Foundation*, 2019); retrieved September 25, 2020 from http://www.heritage.org/index, and International Monetary Fund, World Economic Outlook Database, April 2018, http://www.imf.org/external/pubs/ft/weo/2018/01/weodata/weoselgr.aspx.

2. Julian L. Simon, *The Ultimate Resource 2* (Princeton, NJ: Princeton University Press, 1998), 23-40, 162-197.

3.  *The Story of Stuff*, Referenced and Annotated Script; retrieved September 2, 2010 from http://www .storyofstuff. com/pdfs/annie_leonard_footnoted _script.pdf.

4.  Donald Boudreaux, "Human Creativity: Resources Don't Exist Until Humans Make Them Useful" *The Freeman-Ideas on Liberty*, March 2001, Volume: 51, Issue: 3.

5.  John Stossel, "Government Creates Poverty," *Washington Examiner*, Monday, October 3, 2011; retrieved October 3, 20ll from http://washingtonexaminer.com/opinion/ columnists/2011/04/american-indians -demonstrate -how-government-help-creates-poverty?sms_ss=twitter &at_xt=4dbafffcc9b29ca4,0.

6.  Arthur Brooks, *Who Really Cares: The Surprising Truth about Compassionate Conservatism* (New York, NY: Perseus Books Group, 2007, originally published in 2006 by Basic Books).

7.  "Americans gave $427.71 billion to charity in 2018 amid complex year for charitable giving," *Giving USA 2019*, June 18, 2019; retrieved September 7, 2020 from https://givingusa.org/giving-usa-2019-americans-gave -427-71-billion-to-charity-in-2018-amid-complex-year -for-charitable-giving/.

# CHAPTER 9

# TEST BY LIFE AND DEATH

*Power kills; absolute power kills absolutely.*
—R. J. Rummel

Jesus came to set the captives free and bring abundant *life* to mankind. Satan steals, *kills*, and destroys. The true nature of any philosophy can be determined by examining historical evidence to see what happens when it is implemented. The ultimate test: Does it produce life...or death?[1]

> *The thief does not come except to steal, and to KILL, and to destroy. I have come that they*

*may have LIFE, and that they may have it more abundantly* (John 10:10).

Although socialism and communism had been attempted by small, isolated groups previously, there had never before been a communist government with actual power over the citizens until Vladimir Lenin (1870—1924) came along.

> "Lenin condemned the peasants to be the mere building blocks of the Communist edifice that he had fixed in his mind."

What Karl Marx and Friedrich Engels had proposed in *The Communist Manifesto* was embraced with murderous zeal by Lenin. For the first time, communist revolutionaries became determined to implement communism by force. Lenin, Russian revolutionary, economic theorist, lawyer, and political philosopher who created the Soviet Communist Party, led the Bolshevik Revolution of 1917 in Russia.

Lenin condemned the peasants to be the mere building blocks of the Communist edifice that he had fixed in his mind. It was the peasants who bore the brunt of the civil war. ... This was the path to Lenin's cooperative plan and socialist industrialization. It was for this, according to him, that people were shot in the thousands.[2, 3]

Mass executions, artificially created famines, slave labor and death camps (gulags), and forced migrations of whole racial and ethnic groups were responsible for possibly one million deaths. Lenin's violent and crude language coupled with a total lack of conscience "escalated into the physical elimination of all those who chose not to fall into line, and...once absorbed as normal behavior by the Party, this became an integral and essential feature of the regime in its post-Lenin years."[4] If Lenin had not died at the relatively young age of fifty-three, the numbers of those murdered would certainly have been much higher.

**Joseph Stalin** (1878-1953) succeeded Lenin in power as the Premier of the Soviet Union. Stalin continued and intensified the violent brutality, ultimately bringing the total killed to an estimated 61,911,000. This is more than the total number deliberately killed by governments for all recorded history prior to the 20th century. Stalin continued the practice of deliberately causing *man-made famines.*

The use of starvation later became a standard tool of communist terror. Stalin was responsible for murdering 333,000 men, women, and children by forced starvation alone. The main goal of this artificial famine/genocide was to break the spirit of the farmers and peasants to force them into collectivization. Plus, it's hard to revolt when you are starving to death.

The first century of the modern age was unprecedented in cruelty and horror caused by communists. Communism is clearly based in love for power and love of an ideology—not love for people. Genuine love does not murder people!

> *God demonstrates his love for us in that while we were still sinners, Christ died for us* (Romans 5:8).

### Excerpt from *The Red Plague*
### by R. J. Rummel

How can we understand all this killing by communists? It is the marriage of an absolutist ideology with absolute power. Communists believed that they knew the truth, absolutely. They believed that they knew through Marxism what would bring about the greatest human welfare and happiness. And they believed that power, the dictatorship of the proletariat, must be used to tear down the old feudal or capitalist order and rebuild society and culture to realize this utopia. Nothing must stand in the way of its achievement.

...Government—the Communist Party—was thus above any law. All institutions, cultural norms, traditions, and sentiments were expendable. And the people were as though lumber and bricks, to be used in building the new world.

[T]o many communists, the cause of a communist utopia was such as to justify all the deaths. The irony of this is that communism in practice, even after decades of total control, did not improve the lot of the average person, but usually made their living conditions worse than before the revolution. …Communism has been the greatest social engineering experiment we have ever seen. It failed utterly and in doing so it killed over 100,000,000 men, women, and children, not to mention the near 30,000,000 of its subjects that died in its often aggressive wars and the rebellions it provoked.

…But there is a larger lesson to be learned from this horrendous sacrifice to one ideology. That is that no one can be trusted with power. …The more power the center has to impose the beliefs of an ideological or religious elite or impose the whims of a dictator, the more likely human lives are to be sacrificed. This is but one reason, but perhaps the most important one, for fostering… democracy.[5]

Love does not murder innocent people!

## Democide

R. J. Rummel, late professor emeritus of political science at the University of Hawaii, coined the word *democide,* meaning "the deliberate murder of its own citizens by a government." His entire career was dedicated to researching violence and war, with the goal of finding a solution for war, genocide and democide. According to Rummel's research, six times as many people died of deliberate democide during the 20th century than in all the wars that took place during that period of time.

"It is as though our species has been devastated by a modern Black Plague. And indeed it has, but a plague of Power, not germs."

In total, during the first eighty-eight years of [the 20th century], almost 170 million men, women, and children have been shot, beaten, tortured, knifed, burned, starved, frozen, crushed, or worked to death; buried alive, drowned, hung, bombed, or killed in any other of the myriad ways governments have inflicted death on unarmed, helpless citizens and foreigners. The dead could conceivably be nearly 360 million people. It is as though our species has been devastated by a modern Black Plague. And indeed it has, but a plague of Power, not germs.[6]

---

## Estimated total killed by all tyrannical governments, 1900-1999 = 262,000,000

---

The battle of our time is truly a *war* for economic control. Who would have dreamed that an economic ideology could unleash the most dreadful killing machine in the history of the world? Unfortunately, innocent citizens are considered expendable "building materials" in this war.

Communist governments were responsible for the democide of **169,198,000** men, women, and children between 1900-1999. The actual number is probably much higher. In *The Black Book of Communism*, Stéphane Courtois writes, "[C]ommunist regimes, in order to consolidate their grip on power, turned mass crime into a full blown system of government."[7]

Communists are convinced mass extermination is a "necessary tool" for implementing their ideology. Old and young, healthy and sick, men and women, even infants and the infirm, were killed in cold blood. They were not combatants in civil war or rebellions; they were not criminals. Indeed, nearly all were guilty of...nothing.[8]

---

World total killed by governments
from 1900-1999 = 262,000,000.

---

The **world total** of individuals deliberately murdered by governments between 1900-1999 totals approximately **262,000,000**. The bodies of these victims would encircle the earth more than four times if they were laid head to toe.

---

The bodies of the victims would encircle
the earth more than four times!

---

## Worse than Hitler

What Hitler did in the Holocaust was horrible! Although the communists have semi-successfully distanced themselves from the Third Reich, fascism is very closely aligned with the ideology of communism/socialism. They are two sides of the same coin. "NAZI" is an acronym for the first two words of the National *Socialist* German Workers' Party. Examine the numbers killed in Soviet Russia and China to those murdered by Hitler. The most commonly quoted estimate is 6,000,000 Jews and 14,000,000 non-Jews. Mao and Stalin were even worse.

| Hitler | |
|---|---|
| Jews | 6,000,000 |
| Non-Jews | 14,000,000 |
| **Mao Zedong** (China) | 76,000,000 |
| **Soviet Russia** | 61,911,000 |

Source: R. J. Rummel[9]

## The Killing Fields of Cambodia

Cambodia was in the midst of such a revival that it seemed as if the entire nation would turn to Jesus. However, communism intervened. In 1970, the Khmer Rouge communists who had been fighting guerilla warfare from the hills of Cambodia, took advantage of a coup against their ruler, Prince Sihanouk. They set in motion their murderous plot to take Cambodia back to the agrarian Middle Ages through forcing all citizens onto collective farms.

The Cambodians begged the United States for help, but thanks to American anti-war protests by left-leaning socialist/communist college students, Congress refused.

As a result, the communists took over and, according to the figure taught to Cambodian school children, slaughtered 3.3 million men, women, and children out of a total population of only seven to eight million. One-third of the nation's citizens were slaughtered. Communist thugs swarmed into the cities and marched everyone out. Everyone. Even the sick in hospitals and the feeble elderly, many of whom dropped dead along the roadside.

When they reached the countryside, not wanting to waste ammunition, the soldiers brutally clubbed everyone to death. They viciously grabbed the babies by the feet and smashed their skulls on tree trunks.

The killing fields of Cambodia. Read the books of survivors. They are truly heartbreaking. How could such things happen in a modern, civilized world! One particular young girl lived through the butchery only because so many dead bodies fell on her that nobody could tell she was alive. Hours later, when all was quiet, she managed to crawl out from her bloody tomb and escape.

All this to force an economic policy on an unwilling people.

Why? To break the spirit of a people so they would submit to communism.

Communists don't love people. They love an *idea* and people are merely the building blocks. If some are killed, so what? It's all for the sake of the revolution.

## The Holodomor

During 1932-33, Stalin ordered a man-made famine to crush the spirit of Ukraine. The Ukrainian peasants were individualists who proudly resisted subjugation. For the communists, collectivizing agriculture was a tool of domination. Collectivization is more a political ideology than economic policy—a means of stifling private initiative and gaining total control.

The communists, beginning with Lenin and Stalin, were the first to use the weapon of starvation as a tool to dominate and eliminate people. One horrifying example is the Holodomor, meaning "death by starvation, in the Ukraine during 1932-1933.

> The breadbasket of the old tsarist empire, Ukraine, was now to feed the proletariat of Moscow and Petrograd. Requisitioning quotas were higher there than anywhere else in the Soviet empire. To meet them would have been

to condemn thousands of villages...to certain starvation. ...This policy, which aimed to transform the great sugar- and grain-producing areas into huge collective farms with the peasants as nothing more than agricultural laborers.[10]

---

The Bolsheviks sealed the borders of the nation to starve the citizens.

---

The grain procurement quota (grain taken to supply cities and troops) was raised to an astronomical level, knowing it would cause a grain shortage, which would, in turn, leave the peasants without enough food to survive.[11] When the starvation began, the Bolsheviks sealed the borders of the nation to make it impossible for peasants to escape or food supplies to come in.

Soviet-controlled granaries were said to be bursting at the seams from huge stocks of 'reserve' grain, which had not yet been shipped out of the Ukraine. In some locations, grain and potatoes were piled in the open, protected by barbed wire and armed GPU [Cheka] guards who shot down anyone attempting to take the food. Farm animals, considered necessary for production, were allowed to be fed, while the people living among them had absolutely nothing to eat.

By the spring of 1933, the height of the famine, an estimated 25,000 persons died every day in the Ukraine. Entire villages were perishing. In Europe, America and Canada, persons of Ukrainian descent and others responded to news reports of the famine by sending in food supplies. But Soviet authorities halted all food shipments at the border.[12]

## Eyewitness Accounts

A survivor of the Holodomor, Miron Dolot, describes the horrors of the famine he faced as a young Ukrainian boy in his book, *Execution by Hunger*:

> Thus this monstrous machine of collectivization was set in motion. It ground, it pulled, it pushed, and it kicked. It was run by human beings, and it worked on human beings. It was merciless and insatiable. Once it started, it could not be stopped, and it consumed more and more victims.[13]

The heroic Soviet Communist defector, Victor Kravchenko, wrote of his experiences of life in the Soviet Union and as a whistleblower Soviet official. His 1946 book, *I Chose Freedom*, describes the prison camps and collectivization. He writes:

> Although not a word about the tragedy appeared in the newspapers, the famine that raged ...was a matter of common knowledge. What I saw that morning...was inexpressibly horrible. On a battlefield men die quickly, they fight back. Here I saw people dying in solitude by slow degrees, dying hideously, without the excuse of sacrifice for a cause. They had been trapped and left to starve, each in his own home, by a political decision made in a far off capital around conference and banquet tables.

"They had been trapped and left to starve, each in his own home, by a political decision made in a far off capital around conference and banquet tables."

> There was not even the consolation of inevitability to relieve the horror. The most terrifying sights were the little children, with skeleton limbs, dangling from balloon-like abdomens. Starvation had wiped every trace of youth from their faces, turning them into tortured gargoyles; only in their eyes, still lingered the reminder of childhood. Everywhere we found

men and women lying prone, weak from hunger, their faces and bellies bloated, their eyes utterly expressionless. Yet at the very time these...scenes were being enacted in Ukraine, food was being sent not to the starving but out of the country.

....We knocked at a door and received no reply. ...Fearfully I pushed the door open...into the one room hut. ...The nightmarishness of the scene was not the corpse on the bed, but in the condition of the living witnesses. The old woman's legs were blown up to an incredible size, the man and children were clearly in the last stages of starvation. ...In an adjoining house...a gaunt woman was busy at the stove.

"What are you cooking, Natalka?" Chadai asked her. "You know what I'm cooking," she answered, and in her voice there was a murderous fury. "Why did she get so angry?" I asked. "Because—well, I'm ashamed to tell you. ... She's cooking horse manure and weeds."[14]

Kravchenko continues:

In bed that night, I thought of the new privileged class in the village—the Party and Soviet functionaries who were receiving milk and butter and supplies from the cooperative shop while everyone else around them starved. Slavishly they obeyed orders from the center, indifferent to the suffering of the common people. The corruption of character by privilege was fearsome to behold; these men who only a few years ago were themselves poor peasants had already lost the last trace of identification with their neighbors. ...Some of the peasants might not be able to write, but all of them understood the injustice only too well.

"Socialism," they sneered. "Robbery is a better name for it."[15]

In 2008, Kravchenko's son, Andrew, released a documentary film, *The Defector*, which is an extraordinary chronicle of his father's passion, sacrifices, and ultimate victory in his struggle to expose the crimes of the ruthless Joseph Stalin.

"Socialism," they sneered.
"Robbery is a better name for it."

### Media complicity

The tragedy in the Ukrainian countryside was masterfully disguised by the Soviet propagandists and journalists. European and American media were complicit in the deception. Socialist-leaning intellectuals, such as George Bernard Shaw, who was mentioned in a previous chapter, approved of any means to further the cause of the communists. Communists fully understood the media must be controlled. The British press provided selective coverage, but the Ukrainian famine was almost invisible in foreign newspapers.

Walter Duranty (1884-1957), Stalinist sympathizer and correspondent for *The New York Times*, was a mastermind of the Ukraine "cover up." He was later awarded a Pulitzer Prize for writing lies. "Duranty skirted the truth and had some of the densest and circuitous reporting that could be found. To reporters in Moscow he was known as Walter Obscuranty."[16]

Most journalists in Russia were either too afraid to speak out or in silent agreement with events taking place. Another hurdle, should anyone dare to write the truth, was getting stories past the censors.

> The European and American media
> were complicit in the deception.

### The heroism of Malcolm Muggeridge

Malcolm Muggeridge (1903-1990), a British freelance journalist without fixed position or income, was initially attracted by the ideals of communism, but became increasingly disillusioned. When he heard conflicting reports about Ukrainian food shortages, he became determined to learn the truth about what was happening and, despite a travel ban, bought a train ticket to the Ukraine. Amazingly, Muggeridge was able to get into the country and investigate without official observation.

No one knew his plans and no Soviet officials tried to stop him. If he had been caught, he would have been executed. Muggeridge saw the horrors of villages abandoned, the absence of livestock, emaciated, starving people, and terrified rope-bound peasants who were herded into cattle cars at gun-point.[17]

Starving Ukrainian Family

After witnessing the horrors of the famine firsthand, he disguised his dispatches in diplomatic pouches. Duranty and many other journalists who were communist sympathizers denounced his reports, calling them fabrications.

Years later, Muggeridge was vindicated and his reports proven true.

Malcolm Muggeridge went to Russia believing in the promise of communism, but left believing in the existence of evil.[18]

> *Hear this, you elders; listen, all who live in the land. Has anything like this ever happened in your days or in the days of your forefathers? Tell it to your children, and let your children tell it to their children, and their children to the next generation* (Joel 1:2-3).

A bad harvest indeed!

## "Bad Harvest"

Former Ukrainian President Victor Yuschenko laments:

> [The Holodomor] was a state-organized program of mass starvation that in 1932-33 killed an estimated seven to ten million Ukrainians, including up to a third of the nation's children. With grotesque understatement the Soviet authorities dismissed this event as a "bad harvest."[19]

A *bad harvest* indeed!

## Could It Happen Again?

Larry Grathwohl, an undercover FBI agent who infiltrated the Weather Underground, a group of revolutionary communists, during the 1970s, said that the "most bone-chilling" thing he heard was a comment by Bill Ayers that an estimated 25 million Americans would probably need to be exterminated to overthrow the American government.[20] If 25,000,000 dead bodies were placed head to toe in straight lines across America from the Atlantic to the Pacific Oceans, they would stretch across the nation nearly eight times.

Fear is the foundation of most governments.
—JOHN ADAMS, *Thoughts on Government*, 1776

## The "Freedom Formula" for World Peace

Why do people smile when beauty pageant contestants answer the question, "What is the most important thing the world needs?" by saying, "World peace."? Because everyone knows she does not have a clue what she is talking about, and there is no way she could actually contribute to *world peace.* So, what *can* bring the longed-for world peace to mankind?

The Founding Fathers of America discovered the true answer for peace. Freedom is a right given by God. It leads to economic prosperity, and decreases hunger and famine. Free people do not go to war with other free nations. Free governments do not kill innocent citizens.

The solution is freedom!

**NOTE WELL!** Every genocide and democide of the 20th century was preceded by gun control and the disarmament of the civilian population.

> [The Constitution preserves] the advantage of being armed which Americans possess over the people of almost every other nation...(where) the governments are afraid to trust the people with arms.
>
> —JAMES MADISON, *The Federalist Papers*, No. 46.

> I ask, Sir, what is the militia? It is the whole people. To disarm the people is the best and most effectual way to enslave them.
>
> —GEORGE MASON, Co-author of the Second Amendment during Virginia's Convention to Ratify the Constitution, 1788

### The U.S. Bill of Rights
### Article II

A well regulated militia, being necessary to the security of a free state, the right of the people to keep and bear arms, shall not be infringed.

# Discussion Questions

1. Why are communists such prolific killers?

2. Why is power in the hands of government so dangerous?

3. What is the estimated total killed by Communist governments between 1900-1999?

4. Where did Lenin and Stalin get the idea for mass democide?

5. Why was mass starvation such an effective tool for subduing the citizens of a nation?

6. What conclusion did Victor Kravchenko reach based on what he observed in the Ukraine?

7. Why do you think the media helped hide the Holodomor from the world?

8. Could the same thing that happened in Russian, China, Germany, and the Ukraine happen again?

9. Why did the some of the Framers of the U.S. Constitution insist on including the Second Amendment in the U.S. Bill of Rights?

# Endnotes

1. R. J. Rummel, *Death by Government* (Brunswick, NJ: Transaction Publishers, 2004, originally published in 1994).

2. Dmitri Volkogonov, *Lenin: A New Biography* (New York, NY: The Free Press, 1994), 478.

3. Vladimir Lenin, *Collected Works of V. I. Lenin Completely Revised Edited and Annotated.* (Whitefish, MT: Kessinger Publishing, 1929). Translated by Joshua Kunitz and Moissaye J. Olgin. Originally published 1929 by International Publishers Co., Inc.

4. Volkogonov, 483-484.

5. R. J. Rummel, "The Red Plague," May 1, 2005; retrieved March 23, 2010 from http://www.hawaii.edu/powerkills/commentary.htm.

6. Ibid., 7, 9.

7. Stephane Cortois, et al, *The Black Book of Communism* (Boston, MA: Harvard College, 1999), 2.

8. Ibid., 7, 79.

9. R. J. Rummel, "20th Century Democide," 2002; retrieved May 3, 2009 from http://www.hawaii.edu/powerkills/20th.htm.

10. Ibid., 13, p. 95.

11. Ibid., 13, pp. 159-168.

12. The History Place (2000). "Stalin's Forced Famine 1932-33"; retrieved May 19, 2011 from http://www.historyplace.com/worldhistory/genocide/stalin.htm.

13. Miron Dolot, M., *Execution by Hunger: The Hidden Holocaust* (New York, NY: W. W. Norton and Company, 1987), 14-15.

14. Victor Kravchenko, *I Chose Freedom: The Personal and Political Life of a Soviet Official* (New York, NY: Charles Scribner Sons, 1946), 118-119.

15. Ibid., 30-131.

16. Oksana Procyk, Leonid Heretz, et al., *Famine in Ukraine 1932-1933* (Canadian Institute of Ukrainian Studies, University of Alberta, 1986), 85.

17. Sábado, "Holodomor: Genocide by Starvation," December 10, 2011; retrieved January 15, 2012 from http://talcana.blogspot.com/2011/12/holodomor -el-genocidio-olvidado.html; Malcolm Muggeridge, *The Green Stick*. (Hopkins, MN: Olympic Marketing Corporation, 1982), 257.

18. Malcolm Muggeridge, *Winter in Moscow* (Grand Rapids, MI: Eerdmans Publishing, 1987), xiv.

19. Victor Yushchenko, "Holodomor," Official Website of the President of Ukraine, Victor Yushchenko, 2007; retrieved July 3, 2011 from http://www.president.gov .ua/en/news/8296.html.

20. Larry Grathwohl, "No Place to Hide: The Strategy and Tactics of Terrorism," *Video Documentary* 1982; retrieved August 1, 2011 from http://wn.com/ Larry_Grathwohl on_Bill Ayers_and_the Weather Underground.; Larry Gratwohl, *Bringing Down America* (New Rochelle, NY: Arlington House Publishers, 1976).

# CHAPTER 10

# RINGING THE LIBERTY BELL

America became God's model of freedom for the whole world. The twin blessings of liberty and free enterprise offer hope to oppressed people everywhere. The poem that is inscribed on the base of the Statue of Liberty refers not to immigration but to Lady Liberty's torch lighting the way to the "golden door" of freedom and opportunity. The door is not just America herself, but a freedom formula for other nations to copy. The following inscription was mounted on the lower level of the pedestal of the Statue of Liberty in 1903:

> Give me your tired, your poor, your huddled
> masses yearning to breathe free, the wretched
> refuse of your teeming shore. Send these, the

homeless, tempest-tossed to me, I lift my lamp beside the golden door!

—Emma Lazarus, *The New Colossus*, by

Freedom had been hunted round the globe; reason was considered as rebellion; and the slavery of fear had made men afraid to think. But such is the irresistible nature of truth, that all it asks, and all it wants, is the liberty of appearing.

—THOMAS PAINE, *Rights of Man*, 1791

## The Declaration of Independence

The Declaration of Independence [is the] declaratory charter of our rights, and the rights of man.

—THOMAS JEFFERSON, letter to
S. A. Wells, May 12, 1821.

Because of the Founding Fathers of America, we have an opportunity that few people have ever had in human history—the opportunity to be free. Our Founders did not believe people should live under tyranny. God Himself created all men equal with God-given rights. It is God's plan for men to be free. Jesus Himself said that He came to "set the captives free." The purpose of government is to protect the rights of citizens to life, liberty, and property. The Declaration of Independence emphasizes the authority of a government is granted by the *consent of the governed*. Therefore, the Preamble of the U.S. Constitution begins with the bold words, "*We the People.*"

## PREAMBLE OF
## THE DECLARATION OF INDEPENDENCE

When in the Course of human events it becomes necessary for one people to dissolve the political bands which have connected them with another and to assume among the powers of the earth, the separate and equal station to which the Laws of Nature and of Nature's God entitle them, a decent respect to the opinions of mankind requires that they should declare the causes which impel them to the separation.

We hold these truths to be self-evident, that all men are created equal, that they are endowed by their Creator with certain inalienable Rights, that among these are Life, Liberty and the pursuit of Happiness. *That to secure these rights, Governments are instituted among Men, deriving their just powers from the consent of the governed.*

1.  *Laws of Nature*

    The universal and eternal laws of God (Divine Law) rule over men and nations.

2.  *Nature's God*

    There is one good and omnipotent God (Nature's God) who rules universally and eternally, judging the affairs of men. Because God is good and His law Absolute, it is man's duty to love God and love people.

3. *Self-evident truths*

God has revealed His truths to man and their authenticity is indisputable. These truths are rational, obvious, and morally good.

4. *Equality*

Men are created equal in God's sight, equal in their rights, and equal in the eyes of justice. They should have equal opportunity, but are not guaranteed equal outcomes.

5. *Inalienable rights*

God Himself is the one gives rights to man. No one can take them away or violate them without coming under the judgment of God. Other rights may be created by statute as "vested" rights, but vested rights are not inalienable. They can be altered or eliminated.

6 *Life, liberty, and the pursuit of happiness*

God gave us the right to life, liberty, and private property.

7. *Purpose of government*

The purpose of government is to protect and preserve the God-given rights of citizens.

> ## 8. *Consent of the governed*
>
> No government has a right to exist except by the consent of the people.

---

The purpose of government is to protect the rights of citizens to life, liberty, and property.

---

A free people [claim] their rights as derived from the laws of nature [laws of God], and not as the gift of their chief magistrate.
>—THOMAS JEFFERSON, *Rights of British America*, 1774

And can the liberties of a nation be thought secure when we have removed their only firm basis, a conviction in the minds of the people that these liberties are the gift of God? That they are not to be violated but with his wrath?
>—THOMAS JEFFERSON, Notes on the State of Virginia, Query 18, 1781

The most sacred of the duties of a government [is] to do equal and impartial justice to all citizens.

—THOMAS JEFFERSON, Note in Destutt de Tracy, 1816

*Birth of a free nation.* When the Declaration of Independence was signed in 1776, an extraordinary event occurred in the annals of world history. It was the birth of a free nation. The grand American experiment had begun—to show the world man *can* govern himself!

> We recognize no Sovereign but God, and no King but Jesus!
>
> —JOHN ADAMS and JOHN HANCOCK, April 18, 1775

## Accomplishment of American Independence

### George Washington

> The preservation of the sacred fire of liberty, and the destiny of the Republican model of government are justly considered as deeply, perhaps as finally staked, on the experiment entrusted to the hands of the American people.
>
> —First Inaugural Address, April 30, 1789

### James Madison

> Happily for America, happily we trust for the whole human race, they pursued a new and more noble course. They accomplished a revolution that has no parallel in the annals of human society. ...In Europe, charters of liberty have been granted by power. America has

set the example...of charters of power granted by liberty.

—*Federalist* No. 14, November 20, 1787

## James Madison

This revolution in the practice of the world, may, with an honest praise, be pronounced the most triumphant epoch of its history, and the most consoling presage [prediction] of its happiness.

—*National Gazette* Essay, January 18, 1792

## John Quincy Adams

The highest glory of the American Revolution was this: it connected in one indissoluble bond the principles of civil government with the principles of Christianity.

—Speech, July 4, 1821

*The Liberty Bell.* Bells rang out throughout America to mark the reading of the Declaration of Independence in 1776. Tradition has it that the day the Declaration of Independence was signed, the Liberty Bell in Philadelphia, Pennsylvania was rung. The Hebrew year of Jubilee occurred every fifty years providing restoration of personal liberty and restitution of property. Part of Leviticus 25:10, announcing the year of Jubilee, is inscribed on the bell:

> Proclaim liberty throughout all the land unto all the inhabitants thereof.

*The Constitution of the United States of America.* No nation had ever before forged a democratic republic. The Founders had no model to copy. They knew that The Articles of Confederation had been wholly inadequate during the war. Finally, due to the faithfulness and perseverance of George Washington, the states agreed to call a Constitutional Convention.

The Framers of the Constitution later said it was a miracle that the convention had even taken place, and called the Constitution itself a miracle.

> The happy union of these States is a wonder; their Constitution a miracle; their example the hope of Liberty throughout the world.
> —JAMES MADISON, Outline, September 1829

> It appears to me, then, little short of a miracle, that the Delegates from so many different States...should unite in forming a system of national Government, so little liable to well-founded objections.
> —GEORGE WASHINGTON, letter to Marquis de Lafayette, February 7, 1788

## Now What?

With the foundation of civil government laid, the Founders found it necessary to turn their attention to economics. America was exhausted, depleted, and deeply in debt. The American colonies had been British dependents for over 150 years. They had absolutely no experience in economic development. Financial resources were limited, they had almost no manufacturing capability, and no banks. The Founding Fathers, especially Benjamin Franklin, James Madison, and Alexander Hamilton turned to Adam Smith for a plan.

At the exact time America became a sovereign nation, a strategy for the nation's economy was provided. Smith had observed that government intervention has a detrimental effect on the creation of wealth. However, freedom unleashed individual effort and creativity, because free individuals protected by just laws create prosperous and inventive societies.

> My God! How little do my countrymen know what precious blessings they are in possession of, and which no other people on earth enjoy!
> —THOMAS JEFFERSON, letter to
> James Monroe, June 17, 1785

*Creating wealth.* Wealth is automatically created in a nation when certain conditions are met. These conditions are a low level of interference from the government, protection of private property, and low taxes. Wealth creation requires:

- Low level of government regulation
- Protection of private property
- Low taxes

---

Free individuals protected by just laws create prosperous and inventive societies.

---

## Four Principles of Social Interaction

Smith observed four principles of social interaction that led to prosperity when accompanied by freedom: Healthy self-interest, division of labor, competition, and benefit of society.

### 1. Healthy self-interest

When people are free to make a living under a system of just laws, they strive to succeed, provide for their families, and cooperate with one another. This mutual cooperation is beneficial to everyone involved.

### 2. Division of labor

Quality and efficiency are increased when each worker becomes an expert in one area of production, based on personal interest and aptitude.

### 3. Competition

Competition is an "invisible hand" guiding a free market by competition for resources. No outside regulation of any type is needed because competition automatically improves products and lowers prices.

### 4. *Society as a whole benefits*

Free individuals and free markets create wealth for both individuals and the nation, and raise the standard of living of poor citizens at the same time.

## Back To Your Neighborhood

Do you remember the predicament of your neighborhood in chapter one? Conditions have deteriorated ever since the HOA took control. The economy of the neighborhood has been devastated. Most people no longer work because it just isn't worth it. Wages are low, taxes are high, jobs are scarce. Many people are suffering from depression. Some activists gather secretly in basements to vent their anger.

Finally, it is time for those in power to face election day. No one dared vote the scoundrels out of office for years because they were afraid to lose all their benefits. But now, the HOA has finally run out of everyone else's money. The HOA reneged on their promises. The neighborhood is broke.

People take a good look around at the devastation that used to be their beautiful neighborhood. The formerly manicured lawns are completely overgrown with weeds. The roads are full of potholes. The homes are in desperate need of repair, cars and bicycles are broken down, and most of the shops are boarded up.

## A New Beginning

You and all your neighbors realize that you have been conned! Everyone in the neighborhood rises up, heads to the ballot box, and votes the bums out of office. You elect different government officials committed to re-establishing a constitution and by-laws with checks and balances. Next, with a new government in place, the neighborhood begins to implement a plan to create neighborhood wealth!

### 1. Freedom

The new government follows the Founders' freedom formula and requires self-reliance and personal responsibility on the part of the citizens.

### 2. New Rules

- Private property.
- Everyone must work.
- If you don't work, you don't eat.

### 3. Free Enterprise

The neighborhood adopts the "Adam Smith" economic plan.

- Protection of private property

- Low taxes
- Low level of government control

## Recovery of Your Neighborhood

The following social interaction takes place. Applying Adam Smith's economic principles, the neighborhood begins to recover from satan's failed strategy of socialism.

### 1. Healthy self-interest

Joe starts an auto repair shop in his garage. Joe repairs Mitch and Katie's car. They pay Joe with their home-grown vegetables. Mitch and Katie begin driving to another neighborhood and sell some vegetables. They start a shuttle service for a few people who want to commute to work in other neighborhoods. They earn enough money to pay Joe for repairing their cars.

More and more people begin to earn money, then use that money to start businesses in the empty buildings, and hire employees. Joe is able to hire four assistants and rent a building. Joe is also able to do a minor repair on Karla's washing machine, who then starts a small laundry service in her home. Local home repair and lawn service businesses are launched. More and more people can afford to purchase items locally.

## 2. Division of labor

Kris and Martha start a bakery. At first, they do most of the work, including cleaning. They hire an expert pastry chef and a cake decorator and the word gets out. Their business grows, so they hire someone to deliver wedding cakes and another person to do clean up. That frees up their time, so they spend less time in the kitchen and begin to open franchises in nearby locales.

## 3. Competition

Julia starts a bakery, too. She adds a party planning service on the side, and offers complete party packages in addition to cakes and pastries. Kris and Martha lose some business, so they cut prices on breads and bagels. Julia cuts some prices, too. Customers like lower prices.

Kris and Martha add some tables and open a small sandwich section for lunch. They streamline their production, which cuts their operating costs, so they can lower prices even more. The whole neighborhood enjoys the lower prices and increased options.

## 4. Society as a whole benefits

As more and more businesses open up and hire more workers, the entire neighborhood begins to prosper. New people start moving to the neighborhood and buying homes. New roads are built, old roads are paved, and several rich couples build large new homes. Property value goes up for everyone! The whole neighborhood is glad to welcome them.

Mr. and Mrs. Ritzy enjoy living in the nice neighborhood and spend a lot of money at the local shops. They also want to be a blessing to their community.

The Ritzys open a shelter for abused and disadvantaged women, in addition to becoming major financial contributors for the local hospital. But they don't just give charitable donations. The Ritzys also hire a sizeable staff to work at the shelter and teach job skills to help people get back on their feet.

It is a Jubilee for your neighborhood. You and your neighbors were economic slaves and now you are free!

## Captivity or Freedom

The seed of socialism was planted when sin was introduced in the Garden of Eden...not from God but from *the tree of the knowledge of good and evil* when man began to rely on human reason apart from God. The ripe fruit of socialism wasn't harvested until the 20th century and what an evil fruit it was. Socialism/communism is a total social, economic, political, and spiritual system that calls good evil and evil good. It is not just a difference of opinion, economic theory, politics, or ideologies. The end result is destruction, not paradise.

The great American experiment in civil government and economics, both based in freedom, quickly made America the strongest, wealthiest, and freest nation in the world. The Framers of the Constitution attempted to limit the power of the federal government through checks and balances.

George Mason, the Father of the Bill of Rights, said, *"Considering the natural lust for power so inherent in man, I fear the thirst of power will prevail to oppress the people."* Mason was right. Mason felt that a statement of rights was necessary to curb the bent of government to infringe upon them. The Bill of Rights states what government *cannot* do to citizens.

In his 1989 farewell address, Ronald Reagan stated, *"Man is not free unless government is limited. ...As government expands, liberty contracts."*[1]

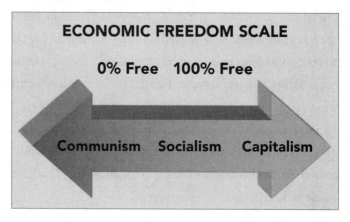

| COMMUNISM | CAPITALISM |
| --- | --- |
| High government control | Low government control |
| High level of entitlements | Low level of entitlements |
| Poverty | Prosperity |
| Captivity | Freedom |

## Who Is a True American?

We must never sacrifice freedom for seductive promises. Now is the time to stand up and be a true American in every sense of the word. A true American is a person who has the same heart and values as the Founding Fathers of America and who cherishes freedom and capitalism for the benefit of all people and nations.

Freedom and free enterprise benefit all people and nations!

## Endnotes

1. T. C. Williams, "Ronald Reagan's Farewell Address," February 6, 2011; retrieved July 26, 2012 from http://republicanredefined.com/2011/02/06/ronald-reagans -farewell-address/.

# BIBLIOGRAPHY

"Americans gave $427.71 billion to charity in 2018 amid complex year for charitable giving," *Giving USA 2019*, June 18, 2019; retrieved September 7, 2020 from https://givingusa.org/giving-usa-2019-americans-gave-427-71-billion-to-charity-in-2018-amid-complex-year-for-charitable-giving/.

Backman, Clifford R., *The Worlds of Medieval Europe,* (New York, NY: Oxford University Press, 2014).

Beck, Glenn, *Arguing with Socialists*, (New York, NY: Threshold Editions, 2020).

Bernays, Edward, *Propaganda,* (Brooklyn, NY: IG Publishing, 2005, originally published 1928).

Bernstein, Eduard, *Evolutionary Socialism: A Criticism and Affirmation,* (New York, NY: Random House, 2019).

Bethell, Tom, *The Noblest Triumph: Property and Prosperity through the Ages*, (New York, NY: St. Martin's Press, 1998).

Biggs, Marcia, "Sick and Starving Venezuelan Children Stoke Fear of a Lost Generation—and More Violence" *PBS*, February 21, 2020; retrieved October 24, 2020 from https://www.pbs.org/newshour/show/sick-and-starving-venezuelan-children-stoke-fear-of-a-lost-generation-and-more-violence.

Boudreaux, Donald, "Human Creativity: Resources Don't Exist Until Humans Make Them Useful" *The Freeman-Ideas on Liberty*, March 2001, Volume: 51. Issue: 3.

Brooks, Arthur, *Who Really Cares: The Surprising Truth about Compassionate Conservatism,* (New York, NY: Perseus Books Group, 2007, originally published in 2006 by Basic Books).

Butler, Ann Caldwell, "Josiah Warren and the Sovereignty of the Individual," *The Journal of Libertarian Studies,* 1980, Vol. IV, No. 4.

Cannon, Caroline, "What Is Free Enterprise?" Investopedia, September 27, 2019; retrieved September 30, 2020 from https://www.investopedia.com/terms/f/free_enterprise .asp.

Cartwright, Mark, "Medieval Monastery," *Ancient History Encyclopedia*, December 14, 2018; retrieved September 16, 2020 from https://www.ancient.eu/Medieval _Monastery/.

Chen, James, "Communism," Investopedia, September 29, 2020; retrieved September 30, 2020 from https://www .investopedia.com/terms/c/communism.asp.

Chol-Hwan, Kang and Rigoulet, Pierre, *The Aquariums of Pyongyang: Ten Years in the North Korean Gulag*, (New York, NY: BasicBooks, 2005).

Clark, Gregory, *A Farewell to Alms: A Brief Economic History of the World*, (Princeton, NJ: Princeton University Press, 2009).

Stephané Cortois, et al., *The Black Book of Communism,* (Boston, MA: Harvard College, 1999).

Conwell, Russell H., *Acres of Diamonds*, (Columbia, SC: CreateSpace Independent Publishing Platform, 2018).

"The Cotton Gin," *Eli Whitney Museum and Workshop*; retrieved July 23, 2009 from http://www.eliwhitney .org/new/museum/eli-whitney/cotton-gin.

"Cuba: 60 Years of Revolution, 60 Years of Oppression," *Human Rights Foundation*, June 18, 2020; retrieved October 26, 2020 from https://medium.com/ @Human_Rights_Foundation/cuba-60-years-of -revolution-60-years-of-oppression-99eedf90f7d2.

Cullen, Jim, *The American Dream: A Short History of an Idea that Shaped a Nation,* (Oxford, NY: Oxford University Press, 2003).

Demick, Barbara, *Nothing to Envy: Ordinary Lives in North Korea*, (New York, NY: Spiegel & Grau, 2015).

DePalma, Anthony, *The Cubans: Ordinary Lives in Extraordinary Times*, (New York, NY: Viking Press, 2020).

Dickinson, John, *The Political Writings of John Dickinson, Vol. I,* (Wilmington, DE: Bonsal and Niles, 1801).

Di Martino, Daniel, "How Socialism Destroyed Venezuela," Economics 21, March 21, 2019; retrieved September 30, 2020 from https://economics21.org/how-socialism -destroyed-venezuela.

"The Division and Specialization of Labor," *Lumen Learning*; retrieved October 23, 2020 from https:// courses.lumenlearning.com/baycollege-introbusiness/ chapter/reading-the-division-of-and-specialization-of -labor/.

Dolot, Miron, *Execution by Hunger: The Hidden Holocaust,* (New York, NY: W. W. Norton and Company, 1987).

D'Souza, Dinesh, *America: Imagine a World without Her*, (New York, NY: Regnery Publishing, 2014).

D'Souza, Dinesh, *The United States of Socialism: Who's Behind It. Why It's Evil. How to Stop It,* (New York, NY: All Points Books, 2020).

Durant, Will and Durant, Ariel, *The Story of Civilization, Vol. X,* "Rousseau and Revolution," (New York, NY: Simon and Schuster, 1967).

Elliott, Jonathan, ed., *The Debates in the Several State Conventions on the Adoption of the Federal Constitution, Vol. 4,* (Philadelphia, PA: Createspace, 2018).

Faria, Miguel A., *Cuba in Revolution: Escape from a Lost Paradise,* (Macon, GA: Hacienda Publishing, 2002).

Fisher, Dan, "The Black Robed Regiment: Preachers Who Fought," *Reclaiming America,* December 20, 2010; retrieved October 28, 2020 from http://reclaimamericaforchrist.org/2010/12/20/the-black-robed-regiment-preachers-who-fought/.

Fleming, John V., *The Anti-Communist Manifesto: Four Books that Shaped the Cold War,* (New York, NY: W. W. Norton & Company, Ltd., 2009).

Friedman, Milton, *Capitalism and Freedom,* (Chicago, IL: The University of Chicago Press, 2003).

Gilder, George, *Wealth and Poverty,* (New York, NY: Basic Books, Inc., 1981).

Garis, Zachary, "The Bible Prohibits Socialism," Knowing Scripture, October 1, 2019; retrieved December 7, 2020 from https://knowingscripture.com/articles/the-bible-prohibits-socialism.

Gower, Ralph, *The New Manners and Customs of Bible Times,* (Chicago, IL: The Moody Bible Institute of Chicago, 1987.

Gratwohl, Larry, *Bringing Down America,* (New Rochelle, NY: Arlington House Publishers, 1976).

Grathwohl, Larry, "No Place to Hide: The Strategy and Tactics of Terrorism," *Video Documentary* 1982; retrieved August 1, 2011 from http://wn.com/Larry_Grathwohl on_Bill Ayers_and_the_Weather Underground.

Gutmann, Ethan, *The Slaughter: Mass Killings, Organ Harvesting, and China's Secret Solution to Its Dissident Problem*, (Guilford, CT: Prometheus Books, 2014).

Harford, Tim, *The Undercover Economist*, (New York, NY: Random House, 2005).

Hayek, F. A., *The Road to Serfdom, The Collected Works of F. A. Hayek, Vol. II*, (Chicago, IL: The University of Chicago Press, 2003. Original text 1944).

Hayek, *The Constitution of Liberty, The Collected Works of F. A. Hayek, Vol. XVII,* (Chicago, IL: The University of Chicago Press, 2011).

Hazlitt, Henry, *Economics in One Lesson: The Shortest and Surest Way to Understand Basic Economics,* (New York, NY: Three Rivers Press, 1988).

Ibrahim, Raymond, *Sword and Scimitar: Fourteen Centuries of War between Islam and the West*, (New York, NY: Hachette Books, 2020).

Ishikawa, Masaji, *A River in Darkness: One Man's Escape from North Korea*, (Seattle, WA: AmazonCrossing, 2018).

Jones, Michael Aaron, "Socialism: The New Feudalism," American Thinker, May 25, 2010; retrieved October 14, 2020 from https://www.americanthinker.com/articles/2010/05/socialism_the_new_feudalism.html.

Kengor, Paul, *The Devil and Karl Marx: Communism's Long March of Death, Deception, and Infiltration*, (Gastonia, NC: Tan Books, 2020).

Kim, Joseph, *Under the Same Sky: From Starvation in North Korea to Salvation in America*, (New York, NY: First Mariner Books, 2016).

Kishtainy, Niall, *A Little History of Economics*, (New Haven, CT: Yale University Press, 2017).

Kravchenko, Victor, *I Chose Freedom: The Personal and Political Life of a Soviet Official,* (New York, NY: Charles Scribner & Sons, 1946).

Lambert, Lance, *Israel: The Unique Land, The Unique People,* (Carol Stream, IL: Tyndale House Living Books, 1981).

Lameiro, Gerard, *Real World Socialism: Spiritual, Moral, and Economic Bankruptcy Sold by Using False Hopes and Deceit*, (Independently published, 2020).

Langlois, Romeo and Benezra, Jorge, "'We're Starving to Death: City of Maracaibo Symbolizes Venezuela's Collapse," France 24, April 24, 2020; retrieved October 26, 2020 from https://www.france24.com/en/americas/20200417-we-re-starving-to-death-city-of-maracaibo-symbolises-venezuela-s-collapse.

Lawson, Robert and Powell, Benjamin, *Socialism Sucks: Two Economists Drink Their Way through the Unfree World*, (Washington, DC: Regnery Publishing, 2019).

Le Bon, Gustave, *The Crowd,* (New York, NY: The Macmillan Company, 1925).

Lee, Hyeonseo, *The Girl with Seven Names: Escape from North Korea*, (London, UK: William Collins, 2016).

Lenin, Vladimir, *Collected Works of V. I. Lenin Completely Revised Edited and Annotated Part 20,* (Whitefish, MT: Kessinger Publishing, 1929). Translated by Joshua Kunitz and Moissaye J. Olgin. Originally published 1929 by International Publishers Co., Inc.).

Levitt, Steven D. and Dubner, Stephen J., *Freakonomics Revised and Expanded Edition: A Rogue Economist Explores the Hidden Side of Everything,* (New York, NY: William Morrow Paperbacks, 2020).

London, Matt, "Venezuela: What Happens when Socialism Fails," Fox News, February 25, 2020; retrieved September 30, 2020 from https://www.foxnews.com/media/venezuela-what-happens-when-socialism-fails.

Majaski, Christina, "Invisible Hand Definition," Investopedia, July 23, 2020; retrieved October 1, 2020 from https://www.investopedia.com/terms/i/invisiblehand.asp.

"Manorialism vs Feudalism" Study; retrieved October 22, 2020 from https://study.com/academy/lesson/manorialism-vs-feudalism.html.

Miller, Terry et al., "2019 Index of Economic Freedom," (Washington DC: *The Heritage Foundation*, 2019); retrieved September 25, 2020 from http://www.heritage.org/index, and International Monetary Fund, World Economic Outlook Database, April 2018, http://www.imf.org/external/pubs/ft/weo/2018/01/weodata/weoselgr.aspx.

Moses, Catherine, *Real Life in Castro's Cuba,* (Lanham, MD: SR Books, 2000).

Muggeridge, Malcolm, *The Green Stick,* (Hopkins, MN: Olympic Marketing Corporation, 1982).

Muggeridge, Malcolm, *Winter in Moscow,* (Grand Rapids, MI: Eerdmans Publishing, 1987).

Newport, Frank, "The Meaning of 'Socialism' to Americans Today," Gallup, October 4, 2018; retrieved September 30, 2020 from https://news.gallup.com/opinion/ polling-matters/243362/meaning-socialism-americans -today.aspx.

Ortiz, Julio, *Escape from Cuba: In Search of the American Dream*, (Independently published, 2020).

Orwell, George, *Animal Farm*, (New York, NY: Signet Classics, 1996).

Park, Yeonmi and Vollers, Maryanne, *In Order to Live: A North Korean Girl's Journey to Freedom*, (New York, NY: Penguin Books, 2015).

Paul, Rand, *The Case Against Socialism*, (New York, NY: Broadside Books, 2019).

Payne, Robert, *Marx: A Biography,* (New York, NY: Simon & Schuster, 1968).

Procyk, Oksana, Heretz, Leonid, et al., *Famine in Ukraine 1932-1933,* (Canadian Institute of Ukrainian Studies, University of Alberta, 1986).

Redleaf, Andrew and Vigilante, Richard, *Panic: The Betrayal of Capitalism by Wall Street and Washington,* (Minneapolis, MN: Richard Vigilante Books, 2010).

Reed, Lawrence, *Was Jesus a Socialist?Why this Question Is Being Asked again and Why the Answer Is Almost Always Wrong*, (Wilmington, DE: ISI Books,

Richards, Jay. W., *Money, Greed, and God: Why Capitalism Is the Solution and Not the Problem*, (New York, NY: HarperCollins Books, 2009).

Riley-Smith, Jonathan, *The Oxford Illustrated History of the Crusades*, (Oxford, UK: University Press, 2008).

Rubenstein, Jay, *The First Crusade: A Brief History with Documents*, (Boston, MA: Bedford/St. Martins, 2015).

Rummel, R. J., "20th Century Democide," 2002; retrieved May 3, 2009 from http://www.hawaii.edu/powerkills/20th.htm.

Rummel, R. J., *Death by Government*, (Brunswick, NJ: Transaction Publishers, 2004, originally published in 1994).

Rummel, R. J., "The Red Plague," May 1, 2005; retrieved March 23, 2010 from http://www.hawaii.edu/powerkills/commentary.htm.

Sábado, "Holodomor: Genocide by Starvation," December 10, 2011; retrieved January 15, 2012 from http://talcana.blogspot.com/2011/12/holodomor-el-genocidio-olvidado.html.

Simon, Julian L., *The Ultimate Resource 2,* (Princeton, NJ: Princeton University Press, 1998).

Skousen, W. Cleon, *The Making of America: Substance and Meaning of the Constitution,* (Albion, ID: National Center for Constitutional Studies, 7th edition, 2009. Originally published, 1985).

Smith, Adam, *The Wealth of Nations, Volumes I-III,* (New York, NY: Penguin Books, 1986, originally published 1776).

Snore, Edvins, director, 2010, *The Soviet Story* [DVD], Latvia: SIA Labvakar.

Sowell, Thomas, *Basic Economics: A Common Sense Guide to the Economy*, (New York, NY: Basic Books, 2015).

Sowell, Thomas, *Intellectuals and Society,* (New York, NY: Basic Books, 2009).

Spencer, Robert, *The History of Jihad from Muhammad to Isis*, (Brentwood, TN: Post Hill Press, Bombardier Books, 2018).

"Stalin's Forced Famine 1932-33," The History Place, 2000; retrieved May 19, 2011 from http://www.historyplace .com/worldhistory/genocide/stalin.htm.

Stossel, John, "Government Creates Poverty," *Washington Examiner*, Monday, October 3, 2011; retrieved October 3, 20ll from http://washingtonexaminer.com/opinion/ columnists/2011/04/american-indians-demonstrate -how-government-help-creates-poverty?sms_ss=twitter &at_xt=4dbafffcc9b29ca4,0.

Stossel, John, "Sweden Isn't Socialist," Creators, January 2, 2019; retrieved September 8, 2020 from https://www .creators.com/read/john-stossel/01/19/sweden-isnt -socialist.

*The Story of Stuff*, Referenced and Annotated Script; retrieved September 2, 2010 from http://www.storyof stuff. com/pdfs/annie_leonard_footnoted_script.pdf.

Tudor, Daniel, *Korea: The Impossible Country*, (Rutland, VT: Tuttle Publishing, 2018).

Thatcher, Margaret, interview with journalist Llew Gardner, Thames television's *This Week* program on November 5, 1976; retrieved July 17, 2011 from http://www .margaretthatcher.org /speeches/displaydocument .asp?docid=102953.

"Tom Paine on the 'Birthday of a New World,'" Online Library of Liberty; retrieved October 23, 2020 from https://oll.libertyfund.org/quotes/381.

Vander Laan, Ray, *Life and Ministry of the Messiah Discovery Guide,* (Grand Rapids, MI: Zondervan, 2009).

Villa, Marina, *Leaving Castro's Cuba: The Story of an Immigrant Family*, (North Charleston, SC: CreateSpace, 2008).

Volkogonov, Dmitri, *Lenin: A New Biography,* (New York, NY: The Free Press, 1994).

Webster, Noah, *An American Dictionary of the English Language,* (New York, NY: S. Converse, 1828).

Wesley, John, *John Wesley's Sermons: An Anthology*, "The Use of Money," (Nashville, TN: Abingdon Press, 1991).

Yueh, Linda, "Friedrich Hayek's Devotion to the Free Market," *Footnotes to Plato*; retrieved September 30 from https://www.the-tls.co.uk/articles/hayek-devotion -free-market/.

Yushchenko, Victor, "Holodomor," Official Website of the President of Ukraine, 2007; retrieved July 3, 2011 from http://www.president.gov.ua/en/news/8296.html.

# ABOUT THE AUTHORS

Drs. Dennis and Jennifer Clark minister together as a husband and wife team and are Senior Pastors of Kingdom Life Church in Fort Mill, South Carolina. They are also founders and directors of Full Stature Ministries and TEAM Embassy School. Dennis holds a PhD in Theology and Jennifer holds a ThD in Theology as well as BS, MS, and EdS degrees in psychology. As an amateur historian, Dr. Jen has a deep love for America and American history.

Visit the authors online at www.forgive123.com.